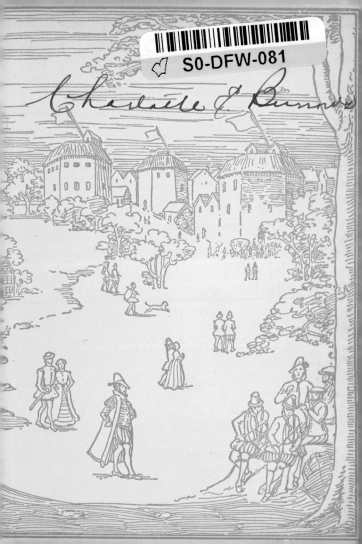

S0-DFW-081

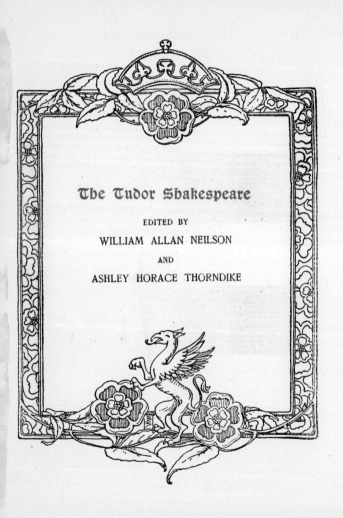

The Tudor Shakespeare

EDITED BY

WILLIAM ALLAN NEILSON

AND

ASHLEY HORACE THORNDIKE

THE MACMILLAN COMPANY
NEW YORK · BOSTON · CHICAGO
SAN FRANCISCO

MACMILLAN & CO., Limited
LONDON · BOMBAY · CALCUTTA
MELBOURNE

THE MACMILLAN CO. OF CANADA, Ltd.
TORONTO

𝕿𝖍𝖊 𝕿𝖚𝖉𝖔𝖗 𝕾𝖍𝖆𝖐𝖊𝖘𝖕𝖊𝖆𝖗𝖊 is published in thirty-nine volumes, including all of the plays and poems, each under the special editorship of an American scholar. The general editors are WILLIAM ALLAN NEILSON, Ph.D., LL.D., President of Smith College, and ASHLEY HORACE THORNDIKE, Ph.D., L.H.D., of Columbia University.

Romeo and Juliet — The GENERAL EDITORS.

A Midsummer-Night's Dream — JOHN W. CUNLIFFE, D.Lit., Professor of English, Columbia University.

Macbeth — ARTHUR C. L. BROWN, Ph.D., Professor of English, Northwestern University.

Henry IV, Part I — FRANK W. CHANDLER, Ph.D., Professor of English and Comparative Literature, University of Cincinnati.

Troilus and Cressida — JOHN S. P. TATLOCK, Ph.D., Professor of English, University of Michigan.

Henry V — LEWIS F. MOTT, Ph.D., Professor of English, College of the City of New York.

The Merchant of Venice — HARRY M. AYRES, Ph.D., Assistant Professor of English, Columbia University.

As You Like It — MARTHA H. SHACKFORD, Ph.D., Associate Professor of English Literature, Wellesley College.

Coriolanus — STUART P. SHERMAN, Ph.D., Professor of English, University of Illinois.

Henry VI, Part I — LOUISE POUND, Ph.D., Assistant Professor of English, University of Nebraska.

Henry VIII — CHARLES G. DUNLAP, Litt.D., Professor of English Literature, University of Kansas.

Comedy of Errors — FREDERICK MORGAN PADELFORD, Ph.D., Professor of English, University of Washington.

King John — HENRY M. BELDEN, Ph.D., Professor of English, University of Missouri.

King Lear — VIRGINIA C. GILDERSLEEVE, Ph.D., Dean of Barnard College.

Much Ado About Nothing — WILLIAM W. LAWRENCE, Ph.D., Associate Professor of English, Columbia University.

Love's Labour's Lost — JAMES F. ROYSTER, Ph.D., Professor of English, University of North Carolina.

Henry IV, Part II — ELIZABETH DEERING HANSCOM, Ph.D., Professor of English, Smith College.

Richard III — GEORGE B. CHURCHILL, Ph.D., Professor of English, Amherst College.

The Winter's Tale — LAURA J. WYLIE, Ph.D., Professor of English, Vassar College.

Othello — THOMAS M. PARROTT, Ph.D., Professor of English, Princeton University.

The Two Gentlemen of Verona — MARTIN W. SAMPSON, A.M., Goldwin Smith Professor of English Literature, Cornell University.

All's Well that Ends Well — JOHN L. LOWES, Ph.D., Professor of English, Washington University, St. Louis.

Richard II — HARDIN CRAIG, Ph.D., Professor of English, University of Minnesota.

Measure for Measure — EDGAR C. MORRIS, A.M., Professor of English, Syracuse University.

Twelfth Night — WALTER MORRIS HART, Ph.D., Associate Professor of English, University of California.

The Taming of the Shrew — FREDERICK TUPPER, Jr., Ph.D., Professor of English, University of Vermont.

Julius Cæsar — ROBERT M. LOVETT, A.B., Professor of English, University of Chicago.

Timon of Athens — ROBERT HUNTINGTON FLETCHER, Ph.D., Professor of English Literature, Grinnell College, Iowa.

Venus and Adonis, and Lucrece — CARLETON BROWN, Ph.D., Professor of English, Bryn Mawr College.

Henry VI, Part III — ROBERT ADGER LAW, Ph.D., Adjunct Professor of English, the University of Texas.

Cymbeline — WILL D. HOWE, Ph.D., Professor of English, Indiana University.

Merry Wives of Windsor — FRED P. EMERY, A.M., Professor of English, Dartmouth College.

Titus Andronicus — ELMER E. STOLL, Ph.D.,

Pericles — C. ALPHONSO SMITH, Ph.D., Edgar Allan Poe Professor of English, University of Virginia.

The Sonnets — RAYMOND M. ALDEN, Ph.D., Professor of English, University of Illinois.

Hamlet — GEORGE PIERCE BAKER, A.B., Professor of Dramatic Literature, Harvard University.

Henry VI, Part II — CHARLES H. BARNWELL, Ph.D., Professor of English, University of Alabama.

The Tempest — HERBERT E. GREENE, Ph.D., Professor of English, Johns Hopkins University.

Antony and Cleopatra — GEORGE WYLLYS BENEDICT, Ph.D., Associate Professor of English, Brown University.

The De Witt drawing of the Swan Theatre in 1596

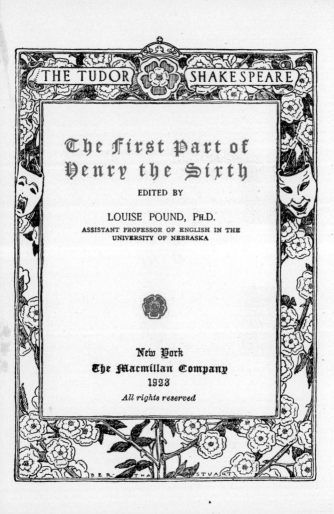

THE TUDOR SHAKESPEARE

The First Part of Henry the Sixth

EDITED BY

LOUISE POUND, Ph.D.

ASSISTANT PROFESSOR OF ENGLISH IN THE
UNIVERSITY OF NEBRASKA

New York
The Macmillan Company
1923

All rights reserved

The Text used is the Neilson Text copyrighted in 1906
by William Allan Neilson

Copyright, 1911

By The Macmillan Company

First edition of this issue of "The First Part of Henry the Sixth"
printed November, 1911

Introduction

Text. — The text of *1 Henry VI* exists only in the form in which it is printed, in 1623, in the Folio of Heminge and Condell. No earlier or unrevised version, such as exists for Parts II and III, is known. The Folio text is in good condition. Whatever irregularities of verse and expression it exhibits are probably not due to external circumstances, but inhere in the play. Blount and Jaggard, who were among the publishers of the first Folio, entered in the Stationers' Register, November 8, 1623, among other copies of plays by Shakespeare, "not formerly enterd to other men," "the Thirde Parte of Henry yͤ Sixt." Since this obviously refers to the unpublished part really belonging first in the sequence, it seems likely that *1 Henry VI* was printed in this year for the first time.

Date of Composition. — When the play was composed may be determined only conjecturally. The diary of the manager of the Rose Theater, Philip Henslowe, records for March 3, 1591-2, the performance of a "new enterlude," "harey vj," on that date. It was acted by the company known as Lord Strange's men, and was repeated many times within the year. Shakespeare undoubtedly belonged to this company; and it seems not unlikely that in the play recorded by Henslowe we have his additions to some older play now made to rest on a new foundation of popularity. Or, *1 Henry VI* may be a play not built on a lost earlier play, but now first composed by Shakespeare, in collaboration with others. It seems safe on the whole to assume the identity of the Henslowe play with the "First Part of Henry the Sixt" printed in the 1623 Folio, although this identity cannot be proved.

An important reference bearing apparently on the Rose Theater play is found in Nash's *Pierce Penilesse,* licensed and published in 1592, who writes: —

"How would it have ioyed braue Talbot (the terror of the French), to thinke that after he had lyen two hundred yeare in his Toomb, he should triumph againe on the Stage and haue his bones new embalmed with the teares of ten thousand spectators at least (at several times) who in the Tragedian that represents his person imagine they behold him fresh bleeding."

Clearly Talbot was a popular figure in a recent play, and probably the special matter referred to is found in *1 Henry VI,* IV. vi-vii. Talbot is the "terror of the French" in I. iv. 42. In Francis Meres' enumeration of Shakespeare's plays, 1598, he makes no reference to a *Henry VI* by Shakespeare; but Meres' negative evidence is of no positive decisiveness. On the whole it cannot be far wrong to assign Shakespeare's work in this play to about the period 1590–1591. In 1590, Shakespeare was but twenty-six, and *1 Henry VI* might well be among the first, if not the first, of his dramatic compositions. The historical order of Shakespeare's plays and the order of their writing need not be the same; but *1 Henry VI* seems earlier in composition than the other parts of the *Henry VI* sequence, and belongs obviously to a younger stage in his dramatic development than *Richard III,* or *King John,* dated usually 1592–1593.

Problems of Authorship. — That Shakespeare is rightly
associated with the authorship of *1 Henry VI* seems established by several pieces of external evidence. His friends
and fellow-actors, Heminge and Condell, printed the play
among his "Histories" in the Folio of 1623. They were
in a position to know whether it counted as his; and there
is no contemporary record that this assignment was ever
called into question. Important also is the testimony of
the final chorus of *Henry V,* 1599, of which the following
are the last lines: —

"Henry the Sixth, in infant bands crown'd King
   Of France and England, did this king succeed;
   Whose state so many had the managing,
   That they lost France and made this England bleed;
   Which oft our stage hath shown; and, for their sake,
   In your fair minds let this acceptance take."

These lines seem to point to a play treating of the crown-
ing of Henry VI as belonging to the larger whole, and, although not decisively, to Shakespeare's authorship of the
whole sequence. Further evidence testifying to his
authorship is the close relation which the *Henry VI* trilogy,
or at least Parts II and III, bears to his play *Richard III.*
Probably then *1 Henry VI* is, in some degree, Shakespeare's; but very few have been able to believe it wholly
his. Its inferiority constitutes no reason of itself for deny-
ing his original or sole composition; but whole tracts of
the play are unlike his known work of this period in dic-
tion, verse, imagery, and general style. There can be for
1 Henry VI, for which an earlier version does not exist,
no elaborately wrought theories of strata in composition,

as for Parts II and III; yet, in view of the Elizabethan practices of recasting old plays and of multiple authorship, there is ample warrant for the assumption that this play, while rightly counting as Shakespeare's, was not his alone.

If *1 Henry VI* represents a rifacimento of an earlier play, possibly a Talbot play, the latter may be the handiwork of some unknown author or authors, and it is futile to inquire who they were. That the play represents Shakespeare's collaboration with or revision of the work of the well-known contemporary playwrights, Greene, Peele, Marlowe, Lodge, Nash, it seems hardly less futile to try to establish. Persistent efforts have been made to distinguish the pen of Greene in Part I; this with no little plausibility. There are some touches like Marlowe, to whom critical opinion is disposed to assign a share in the next parts; though the style of *1 Henry VI* as a whole lacks Marlowe's peculiar vehemence or inflation. Some think that Peele may have written the couplets in Act IV. Yet even if the characteristics in common with these playwrights were far more striking, they might not prove joint authorship with some or any of them, but only their influence. To take positive stand in the parcelling out of the play among possible collaborators, on the precarious evidence of style alone, would be uncritical. All in all, the problems of revision or collaboration are vexing, and not to be solved without light from some outside source.

Which Scenes are Shakespeare's? — Since Shakespeare's is the only name which we may definitely associate with this play, some parts of it must surely be his. Certain scenes stand out as most likely to be from his hand because of their higher poetical quality and clearer resemblance to his known work. Critics are disposed to credit him with the scene in the Temple Garden (II. iv) of the plucking of the red and white roses. The scene of the death of Mortimer (II. v), with its genealogy inserted as if for future purposes, may well be his. Some of the Talbot scenes in IV. ii-vii, and the episode of the wooing of Margaret in V. iii, may be partly or wholly of his composition. Shakespeare was experimenting in the years 1590–1592. His work was more imitative than it was later. Yet readers will find in the scenes indicated verse more harmonious to the ear, more musical and adaptable, than in the main level of the drama. There is more and freer play of imagery, more of the quickness and freshness of spirit that mark the young Shakespeare. Beside showing a more Shakespearean style, these scenes have also more dramatic power.

Sources. — The incidents which form the material of the play were furnished chiefly by Holinshed,[1] Shakespeare's customary authority in his historical plays, and by Halle.[2] For the period of the Wars of the Roses, Holinshed's narrative is a paraphrase of Halle's, and that direct reference was made to Halle is evident from stray touches in the handling. Undoubtedly other sources were used. Perhaps some hints came from Fabyan's Chronicles, or from Stowe. There may also have been reference to

[1] Ralph Holinshed, *The Chronicle of England, Scotlande, and Irelande*, 1577. Second and enlarged edition, 1586–1587.
[2] Edward Halle, *The Vnion of the two noble and illustre families of Lancastre and Yorke*, 1547.

Grafton, whose work is identical with Halle's; indeed Grafton transcribed Halle for the period covered by the play. Whatever the sources, they are treated with great freedom. For instance, the scene of the plucking of the roses has no basis in the chronicles. The dialogue between La Pucelle and Burgundy has no basis in Holinshed or Halle, though possibly drawn from some unknown source. In several places, the Joan episodes are elaborated beyond the chronicle narrative, as in the interview with her father. The Countess of Auvergne episode is another not found in Holinshed or Halle. Verbal indebtedness to the chroniclers is infrequent and of minor importance.

Structure and Style. — *1 Henry VI* is structurally loose; no strong central plan controls the movement. A succession of pictorial scenes, ill strung together, is substituted for the coherent plot structure characteristic of Shakespeare's later historical plays. In the main, the action assumes two forms. There is the external conflict, dealing with the gradual loss of the conquests of Henry V. This occupies nearly two thirds the total number of scenes, and is the part more closely related to the chronicles. The central figures are Talbot and La Pucelle, and the scene France. Coexistent with this foreign or external conflict is the internal conflict, showing the disintegration beginning at home. Through the personal enmities of Gloucester and Winchester, the new political dissensions of York and Somerset, and the youthful incapacity of the King, the Lancastrian sovereignty is weakening to its fall. The drama breaks off with the smouldering factional quarrels ready to flame out. In several link scenes, like the long opening one, or the scenes of the wooing of Margaret by Suffolk, the two forms of the action are brought together, and the inherent relation between them shown. The betrothal of Margaret and Henry is introduced as though to connect this play with the next in the sequence; for the episode has its whole bearing only in Parts II and III. Suffolk's ominous words at the end of *1 Henry VI* sound like a specific introduction to the civil conflict to come, dealt with in the next parts and in *Richard III*.

There are some features in common with the Senecan type of tragedy influential in the early years of Shakespeare's playwriting. The device of messengers who enter to recount disasters is taken from old Senecan tradition. Nearly all the scenes are built on the same model. They end in didactic soliloquy, or in moralizing or prophetic speeches. Thus the first scene of Act III ends with Exeter's speech of chorus-like comment on the discord of the nobles, and he closes the first scene of Act IV with a similar monologue on dissension and division. Prophetic speeches are made by Warwick (II. iv. 124-127), and many other characters. As regards metrical and verbal characteristics, this play has much in common with Shakespeare's earlier work, and reflects the taste of the age. It shows stichomythia, or the rapid succession of speech and reply (IV. v), word and sound repetitions, antitheses and comparisons, the elaboration of conceits, and rhetorical devices of various kinds. The element of comedy seen in the Cade scenes of Part II is wanting in Part I. Wanting also is the element of brutality and horror so prominent in *Titus Andronicus*.

Freedom in the Treatment of Historic Events. — The duration of the historic action is from the death of Henry V, August 31, 1422, to the betrothal of Henry and Margaret, end of 1444. Historic events are treated with confusion and chronological disorder. There are historical errors, events occurring wide apart are massed together, and there are non-historical additions. The loss of Rheims, Paris, Guienne, is antedated. Orleans and Poictiers, reported lost in Act I, were not held by the English when the action of the play opens. Rouen was not regained by the French through the agency of Joan, but long after her death. King Henry is made older in the first part and younger in the last part than he really was. The rupture of Gloucester and Winchester is made to occur at the time of the funeral of Henry V. Talbot is represented as dying before the death of Joan, whereas he really outlived her. The reconciliation of the Duke of Burgundy and King Charles was not caused by Joan, but occurred after her death.

So many are the inconsistencies and repetitions that very careless and hasty revision or collaboration must be assumed. Paris is represented as lost to England in Act I; yet Henry VI is crowned there in IV. i; and, in V. ii, the Parisians are revolting to the French. Winchester is addressed as cardinal in the Tower scene of Act I, yet is still bishop in III. i, and IV. i, and Exeter is surprised that he is installed cardinal in V. i. What the Third Messenger narrates in Act I concerning Talbot's valor " retiring from Orleans," is enacted for us " before Orleans " in II. i. Most puzzling of all are the inconsistent repetitions of the narrative of Fastolfe's cowardice. His flight, in contrast to Talbot's bravery, is recounted in the opening scene, and takes place retreating from Orleans. It is also mentioned by Talbot (I. iv. 35–37). In III. ii, the scene of Act I is specifically enacted, but takes place this time before Rouen. The episode is given for the fourth time in IV. i; but it is here represented as taking place at the battle of Poictiers, perhaps miswritten for Patay, which is the occasion assigned it in the chronicles.

The Characters. — Of Henry VI, the title character, little is seen in Part I, although his weakness and incapacity to control stand out clearly enough. Gloucester and Winchester loom forth among the nobles, but receive fuller treatment in the next part. The hero of the action, so far as there is one on the English side, is the " terrible Talbot." He is pictured as bold yet shrewd, the rough, honorable soldier, devoted to his country. He fights on desperately from battle to battle, with alternating success and failure, until he falls in Act IV, a sacrifice to the rivalries and dissensions of his countrymen. Talbot is joined in his last perilous plight by his young son, and the impressive death scenes of the two, scenes of strong paternal and filial tenderness, strike the one sympathetic human note of the play. Some impulse from Marlowe's *Tamburlaine* may perhaps be recognized in the portrayal of Talbot, an impulse so clearly to be seen in *Richard III*.

On the French side, the most conspicuous figure is Joan La Pucelle. When she first appears, she is drawn with some sympathy, and seems not wholly unworthy of the " holy maid," her country's savior, who rose to be the French national heroine. She is perhaps at her best where her impassioned eloquence wins over the Duke of Burgundy to the French side. Later she is sketched in more wavering strokes, and doubt is cast on her "heavenly mission." At the end, she has become a repulsive figure. She is made to hold communion with fiends, and in a crude and unchivalric scene, built on the chronicles, but dramatically unbelievable, manifests by her own avowals a shamefully degraded character. The chronicles, which reflect the contemporary opinion of her, refer to her variously as a "monstrous woman," a "devilish witch," a "damnable sorcerer." Plainly she was to the authors and their readers a hated figure, the instrument through which the English lost France. No doubt Shakespeare's hearers, perhaps Shakespeare himself, would not have tolerated a favorable picture of her; nevertheless it is pleasing to think that the later Joan scenes are unmistakably from some other hand.

A more consistent figure is Margaret of Anjou, of whom this play gives a first impression. The Tristan and Iseult motive, starting with the wooing of Margaret by Suffolk, as the play closes, is developed into a tragic theme in Part II. Margaret, who appears also in Part III and in *Richard III,* is to prove a fateful central figure and connecting link for the tetralogy.

Relation to Earlier and Later History Plays. — *1 Henry VI* belongs to the stage in the development of the English drama in which the epic chronicle play of the later sixteenth century was in process of transformation into the typical character play which it was soon to become. The early chronicle plays were mere formless agglomerations, showing little attempt at unification of materials. They were marked by allegory and bombast, sometimes alternating with buffoon humor. Only after the lay figures of the earlier plays had been humanized by Marlowe, allegory rejected, and romantic interest added by his freer treatment, did they seem to have much significance or promise. In *1 Henry VI*, crude as it is, may be seen the rising interest in character and the developing realism which were to make, for a few decades, the historical drama so popular a species. It was Shakespeare who was to mould the formless " histories " into clearer outlines, to make them motived and organic, and finally to hold together their loose and diverse interest by interest in the central character. The history play is the type which Shakespeare's genius first developed and first discarded.

1 Henry VI is perhaps read to best advantage when viewed as a " corporate movement " drama. The main interest is not to be found in some private psychological experience, but is distributed among many persons and the whole of which they form a part. A collective or mass interest is substituted for interest in the passional struggle of some definite individuality. Inferior as the play is, it conveys the feeling of far-reaching historical events. The Elizabethan conception of history was crude, and its " true " narratives are a curious blending of the pseudo and the actual; yet it is possible for the reader of *1 Henry VI* to get from it the impression of large movements and to feel, beneath its turmoil and confusion, the real pulse of history.

The First Part of

Henry the Sixth

[DRAMATIS PERSONÆ

KING HENRY VI.

DUKE OF GLOUCESTER, uncle to the King, and Protector.

DUKE OF BEDFORD, uncle to the King, and Regent of France.

THOMAS BEAUFORT, duke of Exeter,
HENRY BEAUFORT, bishop of Winchester, } great uncles to the King.
and afterwards cardinal.

JOHN BEAUFORT, earl, afterwards duke, of Somerset.

RICHARD PLANTAGENET, son of Richard late earl of Cambridge, afterwards duke of York.

EARL OF WARWICK.

EARL OF SALISBURY.

EARL OF SUFFOLK.

LORD TALBOT, afterwards earl of Shrewsbury.

JOHN TALBOT, his son.

EDMUND MORTIMER, earl of March.

SIR JOHN FASTOLFE.

SIR WILLIAM LUCY.

SIR WILLIAM GLANSDALE.

SIR THOMAS GARGRAVE.

Mayor of London.

WOODVILE, lieutenant of the Tower.

VERNON, of the White Rose or York faction.

BASSET, of the Red Rose or Lancaster faction.

A Lawyer.   Mortimer's Keepers.

CHARLES, Dauphin, and afterwards King, of France.

REIGNIER, duke of Anjou, and titular King of Naples.

DUKE OF BURGUNDY.

DUKE OF ALENÇON.

BASTARD OF ORLEANS.

Governor of Paris.

Master-Gunner of Orleans and his Son.

General of the French forces in Bourdeaux.

A French Sergeant.   A Porter.

An old Shepherd, father to Joan la Pucelle.

MARGARET, daughter to Reignier, afterwards married to King Henry.

COUNTESS OF AUVERGNE.

JOAN LA PUCELLE, commonly called Joan of Arc.

Lords, Wardens of the Tower, Heralds, Officers, Soldiers, Messengers, and Attendants.

Fiends appearing to La Pucelle.

SCENE: *Partly in England and partly in France.*

2

The First Part of

Henry the Sixth

ACT FIRST

SCENE I

[Westminster Abbey.]

Dead March. Enter the Funeral of King Henry the Fifth, attended on by the Duke of Bedford, Regent of France; the Duke of Gloucester, Protector; the Duke of Exeter, the Earl of Warwick, the Bishop of Winchester, Heralds, etc.

Bed. Hung be the heavens with black, yield day to
    night!
Comets, importing change of times and states,
Brandish your crystal tresses in the sky,
And with them scourge the bad revolting stars
That have consented unto Henry's death!   5
King Henry the Fifth, too famous to live long!
England ne'er lost a king of so much worth.

Glou. England ne'er had a king until his time.
     Virtue he had, deserving to command.
     His brandish'd sword did blind men with his
         beams;   10
     His arms spread wider than a dragon's wings;
     His sparkling eyes, replete with wrathful fire,
     More dazzled and drove back his enemies
     Than mid-day sun fierce bent against their faces.
     What should I say? His deeds exceed all
         speech.   15
     He ne'er lift up his hand but conquered.
Exe. We mourn in black; why mourn we not in
         blood?
     Henry is dead and never shall revive.
     Upon a wooden coffin we attend,
     And death's dishonourable victory   20
     We with our stately presence glorify,
     Like captives bound to a triumphant car.
     What! shall we curse the planets of mishap
     That plotted thus our glory's overthrow?
     Or shall we think the subtle-witted French   25
     Conjurers and sorcerers, that afraid of him
     By magic verses have contriv'd his end?
Win. He was a king bless'd of the King of kings.
     Unto the French the dreadful judgement-day
     So dreadful will not be as was his sight.   30
     The battles of the Lord of hosts he fought;
     The Church's prayers made him so prosperous.

Glou. The Church! where is it? Had not church-
  men pray'd,
  His thread of life had not so soon decay'd.
  None do you like but an effeminate prince,   35
  Whom, like a school-boy, you may over-awe.

Win. Gloucester, whate'er we like, thou art Protector
  And lookest to command the Prince and realm.
  Thy wife is proud; she holdeth thee in awe,
  More than God or religious churchmen may.   40

Glou. Name not religion, for thou lov'st the flesh,
  And ne'er throughout the year to church thou
   go'st
  Except it be to pray against thy foes.

Bed. Cease, cease these jars and rest your minds in
  peace;
  Let's to the altar. Heralds, wait on us.   45
  Instead of gold, we'll offer up our arms,
  Since arms avail not now that Henry's dead.
  Posterity, await for wretched years,
  When at their mothers' moist eyes babes shall
   suck,
  Our isle be made a marish of salt tears,   50
  And none but women left to wail the dead.
  Henry the Fifth, thy ghost I invocate:
  Prosper this realm, keep it from civil broils,
  Combat with adverse planets in the heavens!
  A far more glorious star thy soul will make   55
  Than Julius Cæsar or bright —

Enter a Messenger.

1. Mess. My honourable lords, health to you all!
    Sad tidings bring I to you out of France,
    Of loss, of slaughter, and discomfiture.
    Guienne, Champagne, Rheims, Orleans,   60
    Paris, Guysors, Poictiers, are all quite lost.
Bed. What say'st thou, man, before dead Henry's
        corse?
    Speak softly, or the loss of those great towns
    Will make him burst his lead and rise from death.
Glou. Is Paris lost? Is Rouen yielded up?   65
    If Henry were recall'd to life again,
    These news would cause him once more yield the
        ghost.
Exe. How were they lost? What treachery was
        us'd?
1. Mess. No treachery, but want of men and money.
    Amongst the soldiers this is muttered,   70
    That here you maintain several factions,
    And whilst a field should be dispatch'd and fought,
    You are disputing of your generals.
    One would have ling'ring wars with little cost;
    Another would fly swift, but wanteth wings;   75
    A third thinks, without expense at all,
    By guileful fair words peace may be obtain'd.
    Awake, awake, English nobility!
    Let not sloth dim your honours new-begot.

Cropp'd are the flower-de-luces in your arms;　80
Of England's coat one half is cut away.

Exe. Were our tears wanting to this funeral,
These tidings would call forth their flowing tides.

Bed. Me they concern; Regent I am of France.
Give me my steeled coat; I'll fight for France.　85
Away with these disgraceful wailing robes!
Wounds will I lend the French instead of eyes,
To weep their intermissive miseries.

Enter to them a second Messenger.

2. Mess. Lords, view these letters full of bad mis-
　chance.
France is revolted from the English quite,　90
Except some petty towns of no import.
The Dauphin Charles is crowned king in Rheims;
The Bastard of Orleans with him is join'd;
Reignier, Duke of Anjou, doth take his part;
The Duke of Alençon flieth to his side.　95
　　　　　　　　　　　　　　　　Exit.

Exe. The Dauphin crowned king! All fly to him!
O, whither shall we fly from this reproach?

Glou. We will not fly, but to our enemies' throats.
Bedford, if thou be slack, I'll fight it out.

Bed. Gloucester, why doubt'st thou of my forward-
　ness?　100
An army have I muster'd in my thoughts,
Wherewith already France is overrun.

Enter a third Messenger.

3. Mess. My gracious lords, to add to your laments
  Wherewith you now bedew King Henry's hearse,
  I must inform you of a dismal fight   105
  Betwixt the stout Lord Talbot and the French.

Win. What! wherein Talbot overcame? Is't so?

3. Mess. O, no; wherein Lord Talbot was o'erthrown.
  The circumstance I'll tell you more at large.
  The tenth of August last this dreadful lord,   110
  Retiring from the siege of Orleans,
  Having full scarce six thousand in his troop,
  By three and twenty thousand of the French
  Was round encompassed and set upon.
  No leisure had he to enrank his men.   115
  He wanted pikes to set before his archers;
  Instead whereof sharp stakes pluck'd out of hedges
  They pitched in the ground confusedly,
  To keep the horsemen off from breaking in.
  More than three hours the fight continued,   120
  Where valiant Talbot above human thought
  Enacted wonders with his sword and lance.
  Hundreds he sent to hell, and none durst stand
      him;
  Here, there, and everywhere, enrag'd he slew.
  The French exclaim'd, the devil was in arms;   125
  All the whole army stood agaz'd on him.
  His soldiers, spying his undaunted spirit,

"A Talbot ! a Talbot !" cried out amain
And rush'd into the bowels of the battle.
Here had the conquest fully been seal'd up,   130
If Sir John Fastolfe had not play'd the coward.
He, being in the vaward, plac'd behind
With purpose to relieve and follow them,
Cowardly fled, not having struck one stroke.
Hence grew the general wreck and massacre ;   135
Enclosed were they with their enemies.
A base Walloon, to win the Dauphin's grace,
Thrust Talbot with a spear into the back,
Whom all France with their chief assembled
    strength
Durst not presume to look once in the face.   140

Bed. Is Talbot slain ? Then I will slay myself
For living idly here in pomp and ease
While such a worthy leader, wanting aid,
Unto his dastard foemen is betray'd.

3. Mess. O no, he lives, but is took prisoner,   145
And Lord Scales with him and Lord Hungerford.
Most of the rest slaughter'd or took likewise.

Bed. His ransom there is none but I shall pay.
I'll hale the Dauphin headlong from his throne ;
His crown shall be the ransom of my friend.   150
Four of their lords I'll change for one of ours.
Farewell, my masters ! To my task will I.
Bonfires in France forthwith I am to make,
To keep our great Saint George's feast withal.

    Ten thousand soldiers with me I will take,   155
    Whose bloody deeds shall make all Europe quake.

3. Mess. So you had need, for Orleans is besieg'd.
    The English army is grown weak and faint.
    The Earl of Salisbury craveth supply,
    And hardly keeps his men from mutiny,   160
    Since they, so few, watch such a multitude.

Exe. Remember, lords, your oaths to Henry sworn,
    Either to quell the Dauphin utterly,
    Or bring him in obedience to your yoke.

Bed. I do remember it; and here take my leave,   165
    To go about my preparation.   *Exit.*

Glou. I'll to the Tower with all the haste I can,
    To view the artillery and munition;
    And then I will proclaim young Henry king.

                        Exit.

Exe. To Eltham will I, where the young King is,   170
    Being ordain'd his special governor,
    And for his safety there I'll best devise.

                        Exit.

Win. Each hath his place and function to attend.
    I am left out; for me nothing remains.
    But long I will not be Jack out of office.   175
    The King from Eltham I intend to steal
    And sit at chiefest stern of public weal.

                        Exeunt.

SCENE II

[France.   Before Orleans.]

A flourish. Enter Charles, Alençon, and Reignier,
*   marching with drum and Soldiers.*

Char. Mars his true moving, even as in the heavens
     So in the earth, to this day is not known.
     Late did he shine upon the English side;
     Now we are victors, upon us he smiles.
     What towns of any moment but we have?   5
     At pleasure here we lie near Orleans;
     Otherwhiles the famish'd English, like pale ghosts,
     Faintly besiege us one hour in a month.
Alen. They want their porridge and their fat bull-
       beeves.
     Either they must be dieted like mules   10
     And have their provender tied to their mouths,
     Or piteous they will look, like drowned mice.
Reig. Let's raise the siege; why live we idly here?
     Talbot is taken, whom we wont to fear;
     Remaineth none but mad-brain'd Salisbury,   15
     And he may well in fretting spend his gall.
     Nor men nor money hath he to make war.
Char. Sound, sound alarum! We will rush on them.
     Now for the honour of the forlorn French!
     Him I forgive my death that killeth me   20
     When he sees me go back one foot or fly. *Exeunt.*

*Alarum; they are beaten back by the English with great
    loss. Re-enter Charles, Alençon, and Reignier.*

Char. Who ever saw the like? What men have I!
    Dogs! cowards! dastards! I would ne'er have
      fled,
    But that they left me 'midst my enemies.
Reig. Salisbury is a desperate homicide;   25
    He fighteth as one weary of his life.
    The other lords, like lions wanting food,
    Do rush upon us as their hungry prey.
Alen. Froissart, a countryman of ours, records,
    England all Olivers and Rolands bred   30
    During the time Edward the Third did reign.
    More truly now may this be verified,
    For none but Samsons and Goliases
    It sendeth forth to skirmish. One to ten!
    Lean raw-bon'd rascals! who would e'er sup-
      pose   35
    They had such courage and audacity?
Char. Let's leave this town; for they are hare-brain'd
      slaves,
    And hunger will enforce them to be more eager.
    Of old I know them; rather with their teeth
    The walls they'll tear down than forsake the
      siege.   40
Reig. I think, by some odd gimmers or device
    Their arms are set like clocks, still to strike on;

Else ne'er could they hold out so as they do.
By my consent, we'll even let them alone.

Alen. Be it so.   45

Enter the Bastard of Orleans.

Bast. Where's the Prince Dauphin? I have news for
       him.

Char. Bastard of Orleans, thrice welcome to us.

Bast. Methinks your looks are sad, your cheer appall'd.
       Hath the late overthrow wrought this offence?
       Be not dismay'd, for succour is at hand.   50
       A holy maid hither with me I bring,
       Which by a vision sent to her from heaven
       Ordained is to raise this tedious siege
       And drive the English forth the bounds of France.
       The spirit of deep prophecy she hath,   55
       Exceeding the nine sibyls of old Rome;
       What's past and what's to come she can descry.
       Speak, shall I call her in? Believe my words,
       For they are certain and unfallible.

Char. Go, call her in. [*Exit Bastard.*] But first, to
       try her skill,   60
       Reignier, stand thou as Dauphin in my place;
       Question her proudly; let thy looks be stern.
       By this means shall we sound what skill she hath.

Re-enter [*the Bastard of Orleans, with*] *Joan la Pucelle.*

Reig. Fair maid, is't thou wilt do these wondrous feats?

Puc. Reignier, is't thou that thinkest to beguile
     me?   65

     Where is the Dauphin? Come, come from be-
       hind;

     I know thee well, though never seen before.

     Be not amaz'd, there's nothing hid from me.

     In private will I talk with thee apart.

     Stand back, you lords, and give us leave a while. 70

Reig. She takes upon her bravely at first dash.

Puc. Dauphin, I am by birth a shepherd's daughter,

     My wit untrain'd in any kind of art.

     Heaven and our Lady gracious hath it pleas'd

     To shine on my contemptible estate.   75

     Lo, whilst I waited on my tender lambs,

     And to sun's parching heat display'd my cheeks,

     God's mother deigned to appear to me,

     And in a vision full of majesty

     Will'd me to leave my base vocation   80

     And free my country from calamity.

     Her aid she promis'd and assur'd success;

     In complete glory she reveal'd herself;

     And, whereas I was black and swart before,

     With those clear rays which she infus'd on me

     That beauty am I bless'd with which you see.   86

     Ask me what question thou canst possible,

     And I will answer unpremeditated.

     My courage try by combat, if thou dar'st,

     And thou shalt find that I exceed my sex.   90

Resolve on this, thou shalt be fortunate,
If thou receive me for thy warlike mate.

Char. Thou hast astonish'd me with thy high terms.
Only this proof I'll of thy valour make,
In single combat thou shalt buckle with me,   95
And if thou vanquishest, thy words are true;
Otherwise I renounce all confidence.

Puc. I am prepar'd: here is my keen-edg'd sword,
Deck'd with five flower-de-luces on each side;
The which at Touraine, in Saint Katharine's
    churchyard,   100
Out of a great deal of old iron I chose forth.

Char. Then come, o' God's name; I fear no woman.

Puc. And while I live, I'll ne'er fly from a man.

    Here they fight, and Joan la Pucelle overcomes.

Char. Stay, stay thy hands! Thou art an Amazon
And fightest with the sword of Deborah.   105

Puc. Christ's mother helps me, else I were too weak.

Char. Whoe'er helps thee, 'tis thou that must help me.
Impatiently I burn with thy desire;
My heart and hands thou hast at once subdu'd.
Excellent Pucelle, if thy name be so,   110
Let me thy servant and not sovereign be.
'Tis the French Dauphin sueth to thee thus.

Puc. I must not yield to any rites of love,
For my profession's sacred from above.
When I have chased all thy foes from hence,   115
Then will I think upon a recompense.

Char. Meantime look gracious on thy prostrate thrall.

Reig. My lord, methinks, is very long in talk.

Alen. Doubtless he shrives this woman to her smock;
Else ne'er could he so long protract his speech. 120

Reig. Shall we disturb him, since he keeps no mean?

Alen. He may mean more than we poor men do know.
These women are shrewd tempters with their
tongues.

Reig. My lord, where are you? What devise you on?
Shall we give over Orleans, or no? 125

Puc. Why, no, I say, distrustful recreants!
Fight till the last gasp; I will be your guard.

Char. What she says I'll confirm. We'll fight it out.

Puc. Assign'd am I to be the English scourge.
This night the siege assuredly I'll raise. 130
Expect Saint Martin's summer, halcyon days,
Since I have entered into these wars.
Glory is like a circle in the water,
Which never ceaseth to enlarge itself
Till by broad spreading it disperse to nought. 135
With Henry's death the English circle ends;
Dispersed are the glories it included.
Now am I like that proud insulting ship
Which Cæsar and his fortune bare at once.

Char. Was Mahomet inspired with a dove? 140
Thou with an eagle art inspired then.
Helen, the mother of great Constantine,
Not yet Saint Philip's daughters, were like thee.

Bright star of Venus, fallen down on the earth,
How may I reverently worship thee enough? 145
Alen. Leave off delays, and let us raise the siege.
Reig. Woman, do what thou canst to save our honours.
Drive them from Orleans and be immortaliz'd.
Char. Presently we'll try; come, let's away about it.
No prophet will I trust, if she prove false.   150
Exeunt.

SCENE III

[*London.   Before the Tower.*]

Enter the Duke of Gloucester, with his Serving-men [in blue coats].

Glou. I am come to survey the Tower this day;
Since Henry's death, I fear, there is conveyance.
Where be these warders, that they wait not here?
Open the gates; 'tis Gloucester that calls.
1. Warder. [*Within.*] Who's there that knocks so im-
periously?   5
1. Serv. It is the noble Duke of Gloucester.
2. Warder. [*Within.*] Whoe'er he be, you may not be
let in.
1. Serv. Villains, answer you so the Lord Protector?
1. Warder. [*Within.*] The Lord protect him! so we
answer him.
We do no otherwise than we are will'd.   10
Glou. Who willed you? or whose will stands but mine?
c

There's none Protector of the realm but **I.**
Break up the gates, I'll be your warrantize.
Shall I be flouted thus by dunghill grooms?

> *Gloucester's men rush at the Tower Gates, and*
> *Woodvile the Lieutenant speaks within.*

Woodv. What noise is this? What traitors have we
here?

Glou. Lieutenant, is it you whose voice I hear?   16
Open the gates; here's Gloucester that would
enter.

Woodv. Have patience, noble Duke, I may not open;
The Cardinal of Winchester forbids.
From him I have express commandment   20
That thou nor none of thine shall be let in.

Glou. Faint-hearted Woodvile, prizest him 'fore me?
Arrogant Winchester, that haughty prelate,
Whom Henry, our late sovereign, ne'er could
brook?
Thou art no friend to God or to the King.   25
Open the gates, or I'll shut thee out shortly.

Serving-men. Open the gates unto the Lord Protector,
Or we'll burst them open, if that you come not
quickly.   [*They rush again at the gates.*]

Enter to the Lord Protector at the Tower Gates Winchester
and his men in tawny coats.

Win. How now, ambitious Humphrey! what means
this?

Glou. Peel'd priest, dost thou command me to be shut
out?   30

Win. I do, thou most usurping proditor,
And not Protector, of the King or realm.

Glou. Stand back, thou manifest conspirator,
Thou that contriv'dst to murder our dead lord;
Thou that giv'st whores indulgences to sin.   35
I'll canvass thee in thy broad cardinal's hat,
If thou proceed in this thy insolence.

Win. Nay, stand thou back; I will not budge a foot.
This be Damascus, be thou cursed Cain
To slay thy brother Abel, if thou wilt.   40

Glou. I will not slay thee, but I'll drive thee back.
Thy scarlet robes as a child's bearing-cloth
I'll use to carry thee out of this place.

Win. Do what thou dar'st; I beard thee to thy face.

Glou. What! am I dar'd and bearded to my face?   45
Draw, men, for all this privileged place;
Blue coats to tawny coats! Priest, beware your
beard;
I mean to tug it and to cuff you soundly.
Under my feet I stamp thy cardinal's hat.
In spite of Pope or dignities of church,   50
Here by the cheeks I'll drag thee up and down.

Win. Gloucester, thou wilt answer this before the
Pope.

Glou. Winchester goose, I cry, "A rope! a rope!"
Now beat them hence; why do you let them stay?

Thee I'll chase hence, thou wolf in sheep's array. 55
Out, tawny coats! Out, scarlet hypocrite!

*Here Gloucester's men beat out the Cardinal's men, and
enter in the hurly-burly the Mayor of London and his
Officers.*

May. Fie, lords! that you, being supreme magistrates,
   Thus contumeliously should break the peace!
Glou. Peace, mayor, thou know'st little of my wrongs.
   Here's Beaufort, that regards nor God nor king, 60
   Hath here distrain'd the Tower to his use.
Win. Here's Gloucester, a foe to citizens,
   One that still motions war and never peace,
   O'ercharging your free purses with large fines,
   That seeks to overthrow religion   65
   Because he is Protector of the realm,
   And would have armour here out of the Tower,
   To crown himself king and suppress the Prince.
Glou. I will not answer thee with words, but blows.
                    Here they skirmish again.
May. Nought rests for me in this tumultuous strife 70
   But to make open proclamation.
   Come, officer; as loud as e'er thou canst,
   Cry.
[1. Off.] All manner of men assembled here in arms
   this day against God's peace and the King's, we 75
   charge and command you, in his Highness' name,
   to repair to your several dwelling-places; and

not to wear, handle, or use any sword, weapon,
or dagger, henceforward, upon pain of death.

Glou. Cardinal, I'll be no breaker of the law ;   80
But we shall meet, and break our minds at large.

Win. Gloucester, we'll meet to thy cost, be sure.
Thy heart-blood I will have for this day's work.

May. I'll call for clubs, if you will not away.
This cardinal's more haughty than the devil.   85

Glou. Mayor, farewell ; thou dost but what thou
mayst.

Win. Abominable Gloucester, guard thy head ;
For I intend to have it ere long.

> *Exeunt* [*severally, Gloucester and Winchester
> with their Serving-men*].

May. See the coast clear'd, and then we will depart.
Good God, these nobles should such stomachs
bear !   90
I myself fight not once in forty year.   *Exeunt.*

SCENE IV

[*France.   Before Orleans.*]

Enter [*on the walls,*] *a Master Gunner and his Boy.*

M. Gun. Sirrah, thou know'st how Orleans is besieg'd,
And how the English have the suburbs won.

Boy. Father, I know ; and oft have shot at them,
Howe'er unfortunate I miss'd my aim.

M. Gun. But now thou shalt not. Be thou rul'd by
     me.   5
     Chief master-gunner am I of this town;
     Something I must do to procure me grace.
     The Prince's espials have inform'd me
     How the English, in the suburbs close intrench'd,
     Went through a secret grate of iron bars   10
     In yonder tower to overpeer the city,
     And thence discover how with most advantage
     They may vex us with shot or with assault.
     To intercept this inconvenience,
     A piece of ordnance 'gainst it I have plac'd;   15
     And even these three days have I watch'd
     If I could see them.
     Now do thou watch, for I can stay no longer.
     If thou spy'st any, run and bring me word;
     And thou shalt find me at the governor's.   20
                             Exit.

Boy. Father, I warrant you; take you no care.
     I'll never trouble you, if I may spy them.   *Exit.*

*Enter, on the turret, the Lords Salisbury and Talbot,
[Sir William Glansdale, Sir Thomas Gargrave,]
and others.*

Sal. Talbot, my life, my joy, again return'd!
     How wert thou handled being prisoner?
     Or by what means got'st thou to be releas'd?   25
     Discourse, I prithee, on this turret's top.

Tal. The Earl of Bedford had a prisoner
    Call'd the brave Lord Ponton de Santrailles;
    For him was I exchang'd and ransomed.
    But with a baser man of arms by far   30
    Once in contempt they would have barter'd me;
    Which I disdaining scorn'd, and craved death
    Rather than I would be so vile-esteem'd.
    In fine, redeem'd I was as I desir'd.
    But, O! the treacherous Fastolfe wounds my
        heart,   35
    Whom with my bare fists I would execute,
    If I now had him brought into my power.
Sal. Yet tell'st thou not how thou wert entertain'd.
Tal. With scoffs and scorns and contumelious taunts.
    In open market-place produc'd they me,   40
    To be a public spectacle to all.
    Here, said they, is the terror of the French,
    The scarecrow that affrights our children so.
    Then broke I from the officers that led me,
    And with my nails digg'd stones out of the
        ground,   45
    To hurl at the beholders of my shame.
    My grisly countenance made others fly;
    None durst come near for fear of sudden death.
    In iron walls they deem'd me not secure;
    So great fear of my name 'mongst them were
        spread   50
    That they suppos'd I could rend bars of steel

And spurn in pieces posts of adamant;
Wherefore a guard of chosen shot I had
That walk'd about me every minute while;
And if I did but stir out of my bed,   55
Ready they were to shoot me to the heart.

Enter the Boy with a linstock.

Sal. I grieve to hear what torments you endur'd,
But we will be reveng'd sufficiently.
Now it is supper-time in Orleans.
Here, through this secret grate, I count each
    one   60
And view the Frenchmen how they fortify.
Let us look in; the sight will much delight thee.
Sir Thomas Gargrave, and Sir William Glansdale,
Let me have your express opinions
Where is best place to make our battery next.   65

Gar. I think, at the north gate; for there stands
    lords.

Glan. And I, here, at the bulwark of the bridge.

Tal. For aught I see, this city must be famish'd,
Or with light skirmishes enfeebled.

Shot [from the town], and Salisbury [and Gargrave] fall.

Sal. O Lord, have mercy on us, wretched sinners!   70

Gar. O Lord, have mercy on me, woeful man!

Tal. What chance is this that suddenly hath cross'd us?
Speak, Salisbury; at least, if thou canst, speak.

How far'st thou, mirror of all martial men ?
One of thy eyes and thy cheek's side struck off ! 75
Accursed tower ! accursed fatal hand
That hath contriv'd this woeful tragedy !
In thirteen battles Salisbury o'ercame.
Henry the Fifth he first train'd to the wars.
Whilst any trump did sound, or drum struck up, 80
His sword did ne'er leave striking in the field.
Yet liv'st thou, Salisbury ? Though thy speech
    doth fail,
One eye thou hast, to look to heaven for grace ;
The sun with one eye vieweth all the world.
Heaven, be thou gracious to none alive,   85
If Salisbury wants mercy at thy hands !
Bear hence his body ; I will help to bury it.
Sir Thomas Gargrave, hast thou any life ?
Speak unto Talbot ; nay, look up to him.
Salisbury, cheer thy spirit with this comfort ;   90
Thou shalt not die whiles —
He beckons with his hand and smiles on me,
As who should say, "When I am dead and gone,
Remember to avenge me on the French."
Plantagenet, I will ; and like thee, [Nero,]   95
Play on the lute, beholding the towns burn.
Wretched shall France be only in my name.
    Here an alarum, and it thunders and lightens.
What stir is this ? What tumult's in the heavens ?
Whence cometh this alarum and the noise ?

Enter a Messenger.

Mess. My lord, my lord, the French have gather'd
head.   100
The Dauphin, with one Joan la Pucelle join'd,
A holy prophetess new risen up,
Is come with a great power to raise the siege.
              Here Salisbury lifteth himself up and groans.

Tal. Hear, hear how dying Salisbury doth groan !
It irks his heart he cannot be reveng'd.   105
Frenchmen, I'll be a Salisbury to you.
Pucelle or puzzel, dolphin or dogfish,
Your hearts I'll stamp out with my horse's heels,
And make a quagmire of your mingled brains.
Convey me Salisbury into his tent,   110
And then we'll try what these dastard Frenchmen
dare.

              Alarum.   Exeunt [bearing out the bodies].

SCENE V

[The same.]

*Here an alarum again : and Talbot pursueth the Dauphin,
and driveth him.   Then enter Joan la Pucelle,
driving Englishmen before her [and exit after them].
Then re-enter Talbot.*

Tal. Where is my strength, my valour, and my force ?
Our English troops retire, I cannot stay them ;
A woman clad in armour chaseth them.

Re-enter La Pucelle.

Here, here she comes. I'll have a bout with thee;
Devil or devil's dam, I'll conjure thee.   5
Blood will I draw on thee, thou art a witch,
And straightway give thy soul to him thou serv'st.

Puc. Come, come, 'tis only I that must disgrace thee.

              Here they fight.

Tal. Heavens, can you suffer hell so to prevail?
My breast I'll burst with straining of my
     courage   10
And from my shoulders crack my arms asunder,
But I will chastise this high-minded strumpet.

              They fight again.

Puc. Talbot, farewell; thy hour is not yet come.
I must go victual Orleans forthwith.

     *A short alarum : then La Pucelle enters the town
        with soldiers.*

O'ertake me, if thou canst; I scorn thy strength. 15
Go, go, cheer up thy hungry, starved men;
Help Salisbury to make his testament.
This day is ours, as many more shall be.   *Exit.*

Tal. My thoughts are whirled like a potter's wheel;
I know not where I am, nor what I do.   20
A witch, by fear, not force, like Hannibal,
Drives back our troops and conquers as she lists;
So bees with smoke and doves with noisome stench
Are from their hives and houses driven away.

They call'd us for our fierceness English dogs; 25
Now, like to whelps, we crying run away.

A short alarum.

Hark, countrymen! either renew the fight,
Or tear the lions out of England's coat,
Renounce your soil, give sheep in lions' stead.
Sheep run not half so treacherous from the wolf, 30
Or horse or oxen from the leopard,
As you fly from your oft-subdued slaves.

Alarum.   Another skirmish.

It will not be.   Retire into your trenches.
You all consented unto Salisbury's death,
For none would strike a stroke in his revenge. 35
Pucelle is ent'red into Orleans
In spite of us or aught that we could do.
O, would I were to die with Salisbury!
The shame hereof will make me hide my head.

Exit Talbot.   Alarum; retreat; flourish.

SCENE VI

[The same.]

*Enter, on the walls, La Pucelle, Charles, Reignier, Alen-
çon, and Soldiers.*

Puc. Advance our waving colours on the walls;
Rescu'd is Orleans from the English!
Thus Joan la Pucelle hath perform'd her word.
Char. Divinest creature, Astræa's daughter,

How shall I honour thee for this success?   5
Thy promises are like Adonis' garden
That one day bloom'd and fruitful were the next.
France, triumph in thy glorious prophetess!
Recover'd is the town of Orleans.
More blessed hap did ne'er befall our state.   10

Reig. Why ring not out the bells aloud throughout the
     town?
Dauphin, command the citizens make bonfires
And feast and banquet in the open streets,
To celebrate the joy that God hath given us.

Alen. All France will be replete with mirth and joy, 15
When they shall hear how we have play'd the men.

Char. 'Tis Joan, not we, by whom the day is won;
For which I will divide my crown with her,
And all the priests and friars in my realm
Shall in procession sing her endless praise.   20
A statelier pyramis to her I'll rear
Than Rhodope's or Memphis' ever was.
In memory of her when she is dead,
Her ashes, in an urn more precious
Than the rich-jewell'd coffer of Darius,   25
Transported shall be at high festivals
Before the kings and queens of France.
No longer on Saint Denis will we cry,
But Joan la Pucelle shall be France's saint.
Come in, and let us banquet royally,   30
After this golden day of victory.   *Flourish. Exeunt.*

ACT SECOND

SCENE I

[Before Orleans.]

Enter a [French] Sergeant, with two Sentinels.

Serg. Sirs, take your places and be vigilant.
    If any noise or soldier you perceive
    Near to the walls, by some apparent sign
    Let us have knowledge at the court of guard.
1. Sent. Sergeant, you shall. *[Exit Sergeant.]* Thus
        are poor servitors,   5
    When others sleep upon their quiet beds,
    Constrain'd to watch in darkness, rain, and cold.

Enter Talbot, Bedford, Burgundy, [and forces,] with scaling-ladders, their drums beating a dead march.

Tal. Lord Regent, and redoubted Burgundy,
    By whose approach the regions of Artois,
    Wallon and Picardy are friends to us,   10
    This happy night the Frenchmen are secure,
    Having all day carous'd and banqueted.
    Embrace we then this opportunity
    As fitting best to quittance their deceit
    Contriv'd by art and baleful sorcery.   15

Bed. Coward of France ! how much he wrongs his fame,
    Despairing of his own arm's fortitude,
    To join with witches and the help of hell !

Bur. Traitors have never other company.
    But what's that Pucelle whom they term so pure? 20

Tal. A maid, they say.

Bed.   A maid ! and be so martial !

Bur. Pray God she prove not masculine ere long,
    If underneath the standard of the French
    She carry armour as she hath begun.

Tal. Well, let them practise and converse with
        spirits.   25
    God is our fortress, in whose conquering name
    Let us resolve to scale their flinty bulwarks.

Bed. Ascend, brave Talbot ; we will follow thee.

Tal. Not all together. Better far, I guess,
    That we do make our entrance several ways ;   30
    That, if it chance the one of us do fail,
    The other yet may rise against their force.

Bed. Agreed. I'll to yond corner.

Bur.   And I to this.

Tal. And here will Talbot mount, or make his grave.
    Now, Salisbury, for thee, and for the right   35
    Of English Henry, shall this night appear
    How much in duty I am bound to both.

Sent. Arm ! arm ! the enemy doth make assault !

                Cry : "*St. George,*" "*A Talbot.*"

                 [*The English scale the walls.*]

The French leap over the walls in their shirts. Enter,
several ways, the Bastard of Orleans, Alençon, and
Reignier, half ready, and half unready.

Alen. How now, my lords! what, all unready so?
Bast. Unready! Ay, and glad we scap'd so well.   40
Reig. 'Twas time, I trow, to wake and leave our beds,
    Hearing alarums at our chamber-doors.
Alen. Of all exploits since first I follow'd arms,
    Ne'er heard I of a warlike enterprise
    More venturous or desperate than this.   45
Bast. I think this Talbot be a fiend of hell.
Reig. If not of hell, the heavens, sure, favour him.
Alen. Here cometh Charles; I marvel how he sped.

Enter Charles and La Pucelle.

Bast. Tut, holy Joan was his defensive guard.
Char. Is this thy cunning, thou deceitful dam?   50
    Didst thou at first, to flatter us withal,
    Make us partakers of a little gain,
    That now our loss might be ten times so much?
Puc. Wherefore is Charles impatient with his friend?
    At all times will you have my power alike?   55
    Sleeping or waking must I still prevail,
    Or will you blame and lay the fault on me?
    Improvident soldiers! had your watch been good,
    This sudden mischief never could have fallen.

Char. Duke of Alençon, this was your default,   60
     That, being captain of the watch to-night,
     Did look no better to that weighty charge.
Alen. Had all your quarters been as safely kept
     As that whereof I had the government,
     We had not been thus shamefully surpris'd.   65
Bast. Mine was secure.
Reig.   And so was mine, my lord.
Char. And, for myself, most part of all this night,
     Within her quarter and mine own precinct
     I was employ'd in passing to and fro,
     About relieving of the sentinels.   70
     Then how or which way should they first break in ?
Puc. Question, my lords, no further of the case,
     How or which way. 'Tis sure they found some
         place
     But weakly guarded, where the breach was made.
     And now there rests no other shift but this,   75
     To gather our soldiers, scatter'd and dispers'd,
     And lay new platforms to endamage them.

*Alarum. Enter an [English] Soldier, crying, "A Tal-
bot! a Talbot!" They fly, leaving their clothes
behind.*

Sold. I'll be so bold to take what they have left.
     The cry of Talbot serves me for a sword ;
     For I have loaden me with many spoils,   80
     Using no other weapon but his name.   *Exit.*
    D

SCENE II

[Orleans. Within the town.]

Enter Talbot, Bedford, Burgundy [a Captain, and others].

Bed. The day begins to break, and night is fled,
    Whose pitchy mantle over-veil'd the earth.
    Here sound retreat, and cease our hot pursuit.

                          Retreat sounded.

Tal. Bring forth the body of old Salisbury,
    And here advance it in the market-place,   5
    The middle centre of this cursed town.
    Now have I paid my vow unto his soul;
    For every drop of blood was drawn from him
    There hath at least five Frenchmen died to-night.
    And that hereafter ages may behold   10
    What ruin happened in revenge of him,
    Within their chiefest temple I'll erect
    A tomb, wherein his corpse shall be interr'd;
    Upon the which, that every one may read,
    Shall be engrav'd the sack of Orleans,   15
    The treacherous manner of his mournful death,
    And what a terror he had been to France.
    But, lords, in all our bloody massacre,
    I muse we met not with the Dauphin's grace,
    His new-come champion, virtuous Joan of Arc,   20
    Nor any of his false confederates.

Bed. 'Tis thought, Lord Talbot, when the fight began,

Rous'd on the sudden from their drowsy beds,
They did amongst the troops of armed men
Leap o'er the walls for refuge in the field.   25
Bur. Myself, as far as I could well discern
For smoke and dusky vapours of the night,
Am sure I scar'd the Dauphin and his trull,
When arm in arm they both came swiftly running,
Like to a pair of loving turtle-doves   30
That could not live asunder day or night.
After that things are set in order here,
We'll follow them with all the power we have.

Enter a Messenger.

Mess. All hail, my lords ! Which of this princely train
Call ye the warlike Talbot, for his acts   35
So much applauded through the realm of France ?
Tal. Here is the Talbot ; who would speak with him ?
Mess. The virtuous lady, Countess of Auvergne,
With modesty admiring thy renown,
By me entreats, great lord, thou wouldst vouch-
        safe   40
To visit her poor castle where she lies,
That she may boast she hath beheld the man
Whose glory fills the world with loud report.
Bur. Is it even so ? Nay, then, I see our wars
Will turn unto a peaceful comic sport,   45
When ladies crave to be encount'red with.
You may not, my lord, despise her gentle suit.

Tal.   Ne'er trust me then; for when a world of men
     Could not prevail with all their oratory,
     Yet hath a woman's kindness over-rul'd;   50
     And therefore tell her I return great thanks,
     And in submission will attend on her.
     Will not your honours bear me company?
Bed.   No, truly, 'tis more than manners will;
     And I have heard it said, unbidden guests   55
     Are often welcomest when they are gone.
Tal.   Well then, alone, since there's no remedy,
     I mean to prove this lady's courtesy.
     Come hither, captain. (*Whispers.*) You per-
     ceive my mind?
Capt.   I do, my lord, and mean accordingly.   60
                                  Exeunt.

SCENE III

[Auvergne. The Countess's castle.]

Enter the Countess [and her Porter].

Count.   Porter, remember what I gave in charge;
     And when you have done so, bring the keys to me.
Port.   Madam, I will.   *Exit.*
Count.   The plot is laid. If all things fall out right
     I shall as famous be by this exploit   5
     As Scythian Tomyris by Cyrus' death.
     Great is the rumour of this dreadful knight,
     And his achievements of no less account;

Fain would mine eyes be witness with mine ears,
To give their censure of these rare reports.   10

Enter Messenger and Talbot.

Mess. Madam,
    According as your ladyship desir'd,
    By message crav'd, so is Lord Talbot come.
Count. And he is welcome. What! is this the man?
Mess. Madam, it is.
Count.   Is this the scourge of France?
    Is this the Talbot, so much fear'd abroad   16
    That with his name the mothers still their babes?
    I see report is fabulous and false.
    I thought I should have seen some Hercules,
    A second Hector, for his grim aspect,   20
    And large proportion of his strong-knit limbs.
    Alas, this is a child, a silly dwarf!
    It cannot be this weak and writhled shrimp
    Should strike such terror to his enemies.
Tal. Madam, I have been bold to trouble you;   25
    But since your ladyship is not at leisure,
    I'll sort some other time to visit you.   [*Going.*]
Count. What means he now? Go ask him whither he
      goes.
Mess. Stay, my Lord Talbot; for my lady craves
    To know the cause of your abrupt departure.   30
Tal. Marry, for that she's in a wrong belief,
    I go to certify her Talbot's here.

Re-enter Porter with keys.

Count. If thou be he, then art thou prisoner.

Tal. Prisoner! To whom?

Count.   To me, blood-thirsty lord;
     And for that cause I train'd thee to my house.   35
     Long time thy shadow hath been thrall to me,
     For in my gallery thy picture hangs;
     But now the substance shall endure the like,
     And I will chain these legs and arms of thine,
     That hast by tyranny these many years   40
     Wasted our country, slain our citizens,
     And sent our sons and husbands captivate.

Tal. Ha, ha, ha!

Count. Laughest thou, wretch? Thy mirth shall turn
          to moan.

Tal. I laugh to see your ladyship so fond   45
     To think that you have aught but Talbot's
          shadow
     Whereon to practise your severity.

Count. Why, art not thou the man?

Tal.   I am indeed.

Count. Then have I substance too.

Tal. No, no, I am but shadow of myself.   50
     You are deceiv'd, my substance is not here;
     For what you see is but the smallest part
     And least proportion of humanity.
     I tell you, madam, were the whole frame here,

It is of such a spacious lofty pitch,   55
Your roof were not sufficient to contain 't.

an occasion requires

Count. This is a riddling merchant for the nonce;
He will be here, and yet he is not here.
How can these contrarieties agree?

Tal. That will I show you presently.   60

*Winds his horn. Drums strike up: a peal of
ordnance. [The gates are forced.]*

Enter Soldiers.

How say you, madam? Are you now persuaded
That Talbot is but shadow of himself?
These are his substance, sinews, arms, and strength,
With which he yoketh your rebellious necks,
Razeth your cities and subverts your towns   65
And in a moment makes them desolate.

Count. Victorious Talbot! pardon my abuse.
I find thou art no less than fame hath bruited
And more than may be gathered by thy shape.
Let my presumption not provoke thy wrath;   70
For I am sorry that with reverence
I did not entertain thee as thou art.

Tal. Be not dismay'd, fair lady; nor misconstrue
The mind of Talbot, as you did mistake
The outward composition of his body.   75
What you have done hath not offended me;
Nor other satisfaction do I crave,
But only, with your patience, that we may

Taste of your wine and see what cates you have ;
For soldiers' stomachs always serve them well.   80
Count. With all my heart, and think me honoured
To feast so great a warrior in my house.

Exeunt.

Scene IV

[*London.   The Temple-garden.*]

*Enter the Earls of Somerset, Suffolk, and Warwick;
Richard Plantagenet [Vernon, and another Lawyer].*

Plan. Great lords and gentlemen, what means this
        silence ?
    Dare no man answer in a case of truth ?
Suf. Within the Temple-hall we were too loud ;
    The garden here is more convenient.
Plan. Then say at once if I maintain'd the truth ;   5
    Or else was wrangling Somerset in the error ?
Suf. Faith, I have been a truant in the law,
    And never yet could frame my will to it ;
    And therefore frame the law unto my will.
Som. Judge you, my Lord of Warwick, then, between
        us.   10
War. Between two hawks, which flies the higher pitch ;
    Between two dogs, which hath the deeper mouth ;
    Between two blades, which bears the better temper ;
    Between two horses, which doth bear him best ;
    Between two girls, which hath the merriest eye ;   15

I have perhaps some shallow spirit of judgement;
But in these nice sharp quillets of the law,
Good faith, I am no wiser than a daw.

Plan. Tut, tut, here is a mannerly forbearance.
The truth appears so naked on my side   20
That any purblind eye may find it out.

Som. And on my side it is so well apparell'd,
So clear, so shining, and so evident
That it will glimmer through a blind man's eye.

Plan. Since you are tongue-tied and so loath to
  speak,   25
In dumb significants proclaim your thoughts.
Let him that is a true-born gentleman
And stands upon the honour of his birth,
If he suppose that I have pleaded truth,
From off this brier pluck a white rose with me. 30

Som. Let him that is no coward nor no flatterer,
But dare maintain the party of the truth,
Pluck a red rose from off this thorn with me.

War. I love no colours, and without all colour
Of base insinuating flattery   35
I pluck this white rose with Plantagenet.

Suf. I pluck this red rose with young Somerset
And say withal I think he held the right.

Ver. Stay, lords and gentlemen, and pluck no more
Till you conclude that he upon whose side   40
The fewest roses are cropp'd from the tree
Shall yield the other in the right opinion.

Som. Good Master Vernon, it is well objected.
　　If I have fewest, I subscribe in silence.
Plan. And I.　　　　　　　　　　　　　　45
Ver. Then for the truth and plainness of the case,
　　I pluck this pale and maiden blossom here,
　　Giving my verdict on the white rose side.
Som. Prick not your finger as you pluck it off,
　　Lest bleeding you do paint the white rose red　50
　　And fall on my side so, against your will.
Ver. If I, my lord, for my opinion bleed,
　　Opinion shall be surgeon to my hurt
　　And keep me on the side where still I am.
Som. Well, well, come on ; who else ?　　　55
Law. Unless my study and my books be false,
　　The argument you held was wrong in you ;
　　　　　　　　　　　　[*To Somerset.*]
　　In sign whereof I pluck a white rose too.
Plan. Now, Somerset, where is your argument ?
Som. Here in my scabbard, meditating that　60
　　Shall dye your white rose in a bloody red.
Plan. Meantime your cheeks do counterfeit our roses ;
　　For pale they look with fear, as witnessing
　　The truth on our side.
Som.　　　　　　　　No, Plantagenet,
　　'Tis not for fear but anger that thy cheeks　65
　　Blush for pure shame to counterfeit our roses,
　　And yet thy tongue will not confess thy error.
Plan. Hath not thy rose a canker, Somerset ?

Som. Hath not thy rose a thorn, Plantagenet?

Plan. Ay, sharp and piercing, to maintain his truth; 70
      Whiles thy consuming canker eats his falsehood.

Som. Well, I'll find friends to wear my bleeding roses,
      That shall maintain what I have said is true,
      Where false Plantagenet dare not be seen.

Plan. Now, by this maiden blossom in my hand, 75
      I scorn thee and thy faction, peevish boy.

Suf. Turn not thy scorns this way, Plantagenet.

Plan. Proud Pole, I will, and scorn both him and thee.

Suf. I'll turn my part thereof into thy throat.

Som. Away, away, good William de la Pole!   80
      We grace the yeoman by conversing with him.

War. Now, by God's will, thou wrong'st him, Somer-
            set;
      His grandfather was Lionel Duke of Clarence,
      Third son to the third Edward King of England.
      Spring crestless yeomen from so deep a root? 85

Plan. He bears him on the place's privilege,
      Or durst not, for his craven heart, say thus.

Som. By Him that made me, I'll maintain my words
      On any plot of ground in Christendom.
      Was not thy father, Richard Earl of Cambridge, 90
      For treason executed in our late king's days?
      And, by his treason, stand'st not thou attainted,
      Corrupted, and exempt from ancient gentry?
      His trespass yet lives guilty in thy blood;
      And, till thou be restor'd, thou art a yeoman. 95

Plan. My father was attached, not attainted,
  Condemn'd to die for treason, but no traitor;
  And that I'll prove on better men than Somerset,
  Were growing time once ripened to my will.
  For your partaker Pole and you yourself,   100
  I'll note you in my book of memory,
  To scourge you for this apprehension.
  Look to it well and say you are well warn'd.

Som. Ah, thou shalt find us ready for thee still;
  And know us by these colours for thy foes,   105
  For these my friends in spite of thee shall wear.

Plan. And, by my soul, this pale and angry rose,
  As cognizance of my blood-drinking hate,
  Will I for ever and my faction wear,
  Until it wither with me to my grave   110
  Or flourish to the height of my degree.

Suf. Go forward and be chok'd with thy ambition!
  And so farewell until I meet thee next.   *Exit.*

Som. Have with thee, Pole. Farewell, ambitious
  Richard.   *Exit.*

Plan. How I am brav'd and must perforce endure
  it!   115

War. This blot that they object against your house
  Shall be wip'd out in the next parliament
  Call'd for the truce of Winchester and Gloucester;
  And if thou be not then created York,
  I will not live to be accounted Warwick.   120
  Meantime, in signal of my love to thee,

Against proud Somerset and William Pole,
Will I upon thy party wear this rose ;
And here I prophesy : this brawl to-day,
Grown to this faction in the Temple-garden,   125
Shall send between the red rose and the white
A thousand souls to death and deadly night.

Plan.   Good Master Vernon, I am bound to you,
That you on my behalf would pluck a flower.

Ver.   In your behalf still will I wear the same.   130

Law.   And so will I.

Plan.   Thanks, gentle sir.
Come, let us four to dinner.   I dare say
This quarrel will drink blood another day.

                     Exeunt.

SCENE V

[The Tower of London.]

Enter Mortimer, brought in a chair, and Gaolers.

Mor.   Kind keepers of my weak decaying age,
Let dying Mortimer here rest himself.
Even like a man new haled from the rack,
So fare my limbs with long imprisonment ;
And these grey locks, the pursuivants of death,   5
Nestor-like aged in an age of care,
Argue the end of Edmund Mortimer.
These eyes, like lamps whose wasting oil is spent,
Wax dim, as drawing to their exigent ;

Weak shoulders, overborne with burdening grief, 10
And pithless arms, like to a withered vine
That droops his sapless branches to the ground.
Yet are these feet, whose strengthless stay is numb,
Unable to support this lump of clay,
Swift-winged with desire to get a grave, 15
As witting I no other comfort have.
But tell me, keeper, will my nephew come?
1. Gaol. Richard Plantagenet, my lord, will come.
We sent unto the Temple, unto his chamber;
And answer was return'd that he will come. 20
Mor. Enough; my soul shall then be satisfied.
Poor gentleman! his wrong doth equal mine.
Since Henry Monmouth first began to reign,
Before whose glory I was great in arms,
This loathsome sequestration have I had; 25
And even since then hath Richard been obscur'd,
Deprived of honour and inheritance.
But now the arbitrator of despairs,
Just Death, kind umpire of men's miseries,
With sweet enlargement doth dismiss me hence. 30
I would his troubles likewise were expir'd,
That so he might recover what was lost.

Enter Richard Plantagenet.

1. Gaol. My lord, your loving nephew now is come.
Mor. Richard Plantagenet, my friend, is he come?

Plan. Ay, noble uncle, thus ignobly us'd, 35
 Your nephew, late despised Richard, comes.
Mor. Direct mine arms I may embrace his neck,
 And in his bosom spend my latter gasp.
 O, tell me when my lips do touch his cheeks,
 That I may kindly give one fainting kiss. 40
 And now declare, sweet stem from York's great
  stock,
 Why didst thou say, of late thou wert despis'd?
Plan. First, lean thine aged back against mine arm;
 And, in that ease, I'll tell thee my disease.
 This day, in argument upon a case, 45
 Some words there grew 'twixt Somerset and me;
 Among which terms he us'd his lavish tongue
 And did upbraid me with my father's death;
 Which obloquy set bars before my tongue,
 Else with the like I had requited him. 50
 Therefore, good uncle, for my father's sake,
 In honour of a true Plantagenet
 And for alliance sake, declare the cause
 My father, Earl of Cambridge, lost his head.
Mor. That cause, fair nephew, that imprison'd me 55
 And hath detain'd me all my flowering youth
 Within a loathsome dungeon, there to pine,
 Was cursed instrument of his decease.
Plan. Discover more at large what cause that was,
 For I am ignorant and cannot guess. 60
Mor. I will, if that my fading breath permit

And death approach not ere my tale be done.
Henry the Fourth, grandfather to this king,
Deposed his nephew Richard, Edward's son,
The first-begotten and the lawful heir   65
Of Edward king, the third of that descent;
During whose reign the Percies of the north,
Finding his usurpation most unjust,
Endeavour'd my advancement to the throne.
The reason mov'd these warlike lords to this   70
Was, for that — young King Richard thus re-
     mov'd,
Leaving no heir begotten of his body —
I was the next by birth and parentage;
For by my mother I derived am
From Lionel Duke of Clarence, the third son   75
To King Edward the Third; whereas he
From John of Gaunt doth bring his pedigree,
Being but fourth of that heroic line.
But mark: as in this haughty great attempt
They laboured to plant the rightful heir,   80
I lost my liberty and they their lives.
Long after this, when Henry the Fifth,
Succeeding his father Bolingbroke, did reign,
Thy father, Earl of Cambridge, then deriv'd
From famous Edmund Langley, Duke of York,   85
Marrying my sister that thy mother was,
Again in pity of my hard distress
Levied an army, weening to redeem

And have install'd me in the diadem.
But, as the rest, so fell that noble earl   90
And was beheaded.   Thus the Mortimers,
In whom the title rested, were suppress'd.

Plan. Of which, my lord, your honour is the last.

Mor. True ; and thou seest that I no issue have
And that my fainting words do warrant death.   95
Thou art my heir ; the rest I wish thee gather,
But yet be wary in thy studious care.

Plan. Thy grave admonishments prevail with me.
But yet, methinks, my father's execution
Was nothing less than bloody tyranny.   100

Mor. With silence, nephew, be thou politic.
Strong-fixed is the house of Lancaster
And like a mountain, not to be remov'd.
But now thy uncle is removing hence,
As princes do their courts, when they are cloy'd 105
With long continuance in a settled place.

Plan. O, uncle, would some part of my young years
Might but redeem the passage of your age !

Mor. Thou dost then wrong me, as that slaughterer
doth
Which giveth many wounds when one will kill. 110
Mourn not, except thou sorrow for my good ;
Only give order for my funeral.
And so farewell, and fair be all thy hopes
And prosperous be thy life in peace and war !

                                      Dies.

E

Plan. And peace, no war, befall thy parting soul ! 115
     In prison hast thou spent a pilgrimage
     And like a hermit overpass'd thy days.
     Well, I will lock his counsel in my breast ;
     And what I do imagine, let that rest.
     Keepers, convey him hence, and I myself   120
     Will see his burial better than his life.

             Exeunt [Gaolers, bearing out the body of
                Mortimer].

     Here dies the dusky torch of Mortimer,
     Chok'd with ambition of the meaner sort ;
     And for those wrongs, those bitter injuries
     Which Somerset hath offer'd to my house,   125
     I doubt not but with honour to redress.
     And therefore haste I to the parliament,
     Either to be restored to my blood,
     Or make my ill the advantage of my good.

                                       Exit.

ACT THIRD

SCENE I

[*London. The Parliament-house.*]

Flourish. Enter King, Exeter, Gloucester, Warwick, Somerset, and Suffolk; the Bishop of Winchester, Richard Plantagenet [and others]. Gloucester offers to put up a bill; Winchester snatches it, and tears it.

Win. Com'st thou with deep premeditated lines,
  With written pamphlets studiously devis'd,
  Humphrey of Gloucester? If thou canst accuse,
  Or aught intend'st to lay unto my charge,
  Do it without invention, suddenly;   5
  As I with sudden and extemporal speech
  Purpose to answer what thou canst object.
Glou. Presumptuous priest! this place commands my
      patience,
  Or thou shouldst find thou hast dishonour'd me.
  Think not, although in writing I preferr'd   10
  The manner of thy vile outrageous crimes,
  That therefore I have forg'd, or am not able
  Verbatim to rehearse the method of my pen.
  No, prelate; such is thy audacious wickedness,
  Thy lewd, pestiferous, and dissentious pranks,   15

51

As very infants prattle of thy pride.
Thou art a most pernicious usurer,
Froward by nature, enemy to peace;
Lascivious, wanton, more than well beseems
A man of thy profession and degree;   20
And for thy treachery, what's more manifest?
In that thou laid'st a trap to take my life,
As well at London Bridge as at the Tower.
Beside, I fear me, if thy thoughts were sifted,
The King, thy sovereign, is not quite exempt   25
From envious malice of thy swelling heart.

Win. Gloucester, I do defy thee.   Lords, vouchsafe
To give me hearing what I shall reply.
If I were covetous, ambitious, or perverse,
As he will have me, how am I so poor?   30
Or how haps it I seek not to advance
Or raise myself, but keep my wonted calling?
And for dissension, who preferreth peace
More than I do? — except I be provok'd.
No, my good lords, it is not that offends;   35
It is not that that hath incens'd the Duke.
It is because no one should sway but he,
No one but he should be about the King;
And that engenders thunder in his breast
And makes him roar these accusations forth.   40
But he shall know I am as good —

Glou.   As good!
Thou bastard of my grandfather!

Win. Ay, lordly sir; for what are you, I pray,
    But one imperious in another's throne?

Glou. Am I not Protector, saucy priest?   45

Win. And am not I a prelate of the Church?

Glou. Yes, as an outlaw in a castle keeps
    And useth it to patronage his theft.

Win. Unreverent Gloucester!

Glou.   Thou art reverend
    Touching thy spiritual function, not thy life.   50

Win. Rome shall remedy this.

War.   Roam thither, then.

[*Som.*] My lord, it were your duty to forbear.

[*War.*] Ay, see the Bishop be not overborne.

Som. Methinks my lord should be religious
    And know the office that belongs to such.   55

War. Methinks his lordship should be humbler;
    It fitteth not a prelate so to plead.

Som. Yes, when his holy state is touch'd so near.

War. State holy or unhallow'd, what of that?
    Is not his Grace Protector to the King?   60

Plan. [*Aside.*] Plantagenet, I see, must hold his tongue,
    Lest it be said, "Speak, sirrah, when you should;
    Must your bold verdict enter talk with lords?"
    Else would I have a fling at Winchester.

King. Uncles of Gloucester and of Winchester,   65
    The special watchmen of our English weal,
    I would prevail, if prayers might prevail,
    To join your hearts in love and amity.

O, what a scandal is it to our crown,
That two such noble peers as ye should jar!   70
Believe me, lords, my tender years can tell
Civil dissension is a viperous worm
That gnaws the bowels of the commonwealth.

A noise within, "Down with the tawny-coats!"

What tumult's this?
War.   An uproar, I dare warrant,
Begun through malice of the Bishop's men.   75

A noise again, "Stones! stones!"

Enter the Mayor [of London, attended].

May. O, my good lords, and virtuous Henry,
Pity the city of London, pity us!
The Bishop and the Duke of Gloucester's men,
Forbidden late to carry any weapon,
Have fill'd their pockets full of pebble stones   80
And banding themselves in contrary parts
Do pelt so fast at one another's pate
That many have their giddy brains knock'd out.
Our windows are broke down in every street
And we for fear compell'd to shut our shops.   85

*Enter [Serving-men of both parties,] in skirmish, with
bloody pates.*

King. We charge you, on allegiance to ourself,

To hold your slaught'ring hands and keep the peace.
Pray, uncle Gloucester, mitigate this strife.

1. Serv. Nay, if we be forbidden stones, we'll fall to
it with our teeth.　　　　　　　　　　　　　90

2. Serv. Do what ye dare, we are as resolute.

　　　　　　　　　　　　　Skirmish again.

Glou. You of my household, leave this peevish broil
And set this unaccustom'd fight aside.

3. Serv. My lord, we know your Grace to be a man
Just and upright; and, for your royal birth,　　95
Inferior to none but to his Majesty:
And ere that we will suffer such a prince,
So kind a father of the commonweal,
To be disgraced by an inkhorn mate,
We and our wives and children all will fight　　100
And have our bodies slaught'red by thy foes.

1. Serv. Ay, and the very parings of our nails
Shall pitch a field when we are dead.

　　　　　　　　　　　　　Begin again.

Glou.　　　　　　　　　Stay, stay, I say!
And if you love me, as you say you do,
Let me persuade you to forbear a while.　　　105

King. O, how this discord doth afflict my soul!
Can you, my Lord of Winchester, behold
My sighs and tears and will not once relent?
Who should be pitiful, if you be not?
Or who should study to prefer a peace,　　　110
If holy churchmen take delight in broils?

War. Yield, my Lord Protector; yield, Winchester;
    Except you mean with obstinate repulse
    To slay your sovereign and destroy the realm.
    You see what mischief and what murder too   115
    Hath been enacted through your enmity.
    Then be at peace, except ye thirst for blood.

Win. He shall submit, or I will never yield.

Glou. Compassion on the King commands me stoop;
    Or I would see his heart out, ere the priest   120
    Should ever get that privilege of me.

War. Behold, my Lord of Winchester, the Duke
    Hath banish'd moody discontented fury,
    As by his smoothed brows it doth appear.
    Why look you still so stern and tragical?   125

Glou. Here, Winchester, I offer thee my hand.

King. Fie, uncle Beaufort! I have heard you preach
    That malice was a great and grievous sin;
    And will not you maintain the thing you teach,
    But prove a chief offender in the same?   130

War. Sweet king! the Bishop hath a kindly gird.
    For shame, my Lord of Winchester, relent!
    What, shall a child instruct you what to do?

Win. Well, Duke of Gloucester, I will yield to thee;
    Love for thy love and hand for hand I give.   135

Glou. [*Aside.*] Ay, but, I fear me, with a hollow
        heart. —
    See here, my friends and loving countrymen,
    This token serveth for a flag of truce

Betwixt ourselves and all our followers.

So help me God, as I dissemble not !   140

Win. [*Aside.*] So help me God, as I intend it not !

King. O loving uncle, kind Duke of Gloucester,

How joyful am I made by this contract !

Away, my masters ! trouble us no more ;   144

But join in friendship, as your lords have done.

1. Serv. Content ; I'll to the surgeon's.

2. Serv.   And so will I.

3. Serv. And I will see what physic the tavern af-

fords.

                        Exeunt [*Serving-men, Mayor, etc.*].

War. Accept this scroll, most gracious sovereign,

Which in the right of Richard Plantagenet   150

We do exhibit to your Majesty.

Glou. Well urg'd, my Lord of Warwick ; for, sweet

prince,

An if your Grace mark every circumstance,

You have great reason to do Richard right ;

Especially for those occasions   155

At Eltham Place I told your Majesty.

King. And those occasions, uncle, were of force.

Therefore, my loving lords, our pleasure is

That Richard be restored to his blood.

War. Let Richard be restored to his blood ;   160

So shall his father's wrongs be recompens'd.

Win. As will the rest, so willeth Winchester.

King. If Richard will be true, not that alone

But all the whole inheritance I give
That doth belong unto the house of York,   165
From whence you spring by lineal descent.

Plan. Thy humble servant vows obedience
And humble service till the point of death.

King. Stoop then and set your knee against my foot;
And, in reguerdon of that duty done,   170
I gird thee with the valiant sword of York.
Rise, Richard, like a true Plantagenet,
And rise created princely Duke of York.

Plan. And so thrive Richard as thy foes may fall!
And as my duty springs, so perish they   175
That grudge one thought against your Majesty!

All. Welcome, high prince, the mighty Duke of York!

Som. [*Aside.*] Perish, base prince, ignoble Duke of
York!

Glou. Now will it best avail your Majesty
To cross the seas and to be crown'd in France. 180
The presence of a king engenders love
Amongst his subjects and his loyal friends,
As it disanimates his enemies.

King. When Gloucester says the word, King Henry
goes;
For friendly counsel cuts off many foes.   185

Glou. Your ships already are in readiness.

Sennet.   Flourish.   Exeunt [all but Exeter].

Exe. Ay, we may march in England or in France,
Not seeing what is likely to ensue.

This late dissension grown betwixt the peers
Burns under feigned ashes of forg'd love,   190
And will at last break out into a flame:
As fest'red members rot but by degree,
Till bones and flesh and sinews fall away,
So will this base and envious discord breed.
And now I fear that fatal prophecy   195
Which in the time of Henry named the Fifth
Was in the mouth of every sucking babe,
That Henry born at Monmouth should win all,
And Henry born at Windsor lose all.
Which is so plain that Exeter doth wish   200
His days may finish ere that hapless time.

Exit.

SCENE II

[France.   Before Rouen.]

*Enter La Pucelle disguised, with four Soldiers with sacks
upon their backs.*

Puc. These are the city gates, the gates of Rouen,
    Through which our policy must make a breach.
    Take heed, be wary how you place your words;
    Talk like the vulgar sort of market men
    That come to gather money for their corn.   5
    If we have entrance, as I hope we shall,
    And that we find the slothful watch but weak,
    I'll by a sign give notice to our friends,
    That Charles the Dauphin may encounter them.

1. Sol.　Our sacks shall be a mean to sack the city,　10
　　　And we be lords and rulers over Rouen ;
　　　Therefore we'll knock.　　　　　　　*Knock.*
Watch.　[*Within.*] *Qui est là ?*
Puc.　*Paysans, pauvres gens de France ;*
　　　Poor market folks that come to sell their corn.　15
Watch.　Enter, go in ; the market bell is rung.
Puc.　Now, Rouen, I'll shake thy bulwarks to the
　　　ground.　　　　　　　*Exeunt* [*to the town*].

Enter Charles, the Bastard of Orleans, Alençon [*Reignier,
and forces*].

Char.　Saint Denis bless this happy stratagem !
　　　And once again we'll sleep secure in Rouen.
Bast.　Here ent'red Pucelle and her practisants.　20
　　　Now she is there, how will she specify
　　　Where is the best and safest passage in ?
Reig.　By thrusting out a torch from yonder tower ;
　　　Which, once discern'd, shows that her meaning is,
　　　No way to that, for weakness, which she ent'red.　25

Enter La Pucelle on the top, thrusting out a torch burning.

Puc.　Behold, this is the happy wedding torch
　　　That joineth Rouen unto her countrymen,
　　　But burning fatal to the Talbotites !　　　［*Exit.*]
Bast.　See, noble Charles, the beacon of our friend ;
　　　The burning torch in yonder turret stands.　30

Char. Now shine it like a comet of revenge,
    A prophet to the fall of all our foes!
Reig. Defer no time, delays have dangerous ends.
    Enter, and cry "The Dauphin!" presently,
    And then do execution on the watch.   35
                  Alarum. [*Exeunt.*]

    An alarum.   Enter Talbot in an excursion.

Tal. France, thou shalt rue this treason with thy tears,
    If Talbot but survive thy treachery.
    Pucelle, that witch, that damned sorceress,
    Hath wrought this hellish mischief unawares,
    That hardly we escap'd the pride of France.   40
                        Exit.

*An alarum: excursions. Bedford, brought in sick in a
    chair. Enter Talbot and Burgundy without: within
    La Pucelle, Charles, Bastard, [Alençon,] and Reig-
    nier, on the walls.*

Puc. Good morrow, gallants! want ye corn for bread?
    I think the Duke of Burgundy will fast
    Before he'll buy again at such a rate.
    'Twas full of darnel; do you like the taste?
Bur. Scoff on, vile fiend and shameless courtezan! 45
    I trust ere long to choke thee with thine own
    And make thee curse the harvest of that corn.

Char. Your Grace may starve perhaps before that time.

Bed. O, let no words, but deeds, revenge this treason !

Puc. What will you do, good grey-beard ? Break a
   lance,   50
  And run a tilt at Death within a chair ?

Tal. Foul fiend of France, and hag of all despite,
  Encompass'd with thy lustful paramours !
  Becomes it thee to taunt his valiant age
  And twit with cowardice a man half dead ? 55
  Damsel, I'll have a bout with you again,
  Or else let Talbot perish with this shame.

Puc. Are ye so hot, sir ? Yet, Pucelle, hold thy peace ;
  If Talbot do but thunder, rain will follow.
     The English whisper together in council.
  God speed the parliament ! Who shall be the
    speaker ?   60

Tal. Dare ye come forth and meet us in the field ?

Puc. Belike your lordship takes us then for fools,
  To try if that our own be ours or no.

Tal. I speak not to that railing Hecate,
  But unto thee, Alençon, and the rest. 65
  Will ye, like soldiers, come and fight it out ?

Alen. Signior, no.

Tal. Signior, hang ! Base muleteers of France !
  Like peasant foot-boys do they keep the walls
  And dare not take up arms like gentlemen. 70

Puc. Away, captains ! let's get us from the walls
  For Talbot means no goodness by his looks.

God b'uy, my lord! we came but to tell you
That we are here.

>   *Exeunt [La Pucelle, etc.,] from the walls.*

Tal. And there will we be too, ere it be long,   75
Or else reproach be Talbot's greatest fame!
Vow, Burgundy, by honour of thy house,
Prick'd on by public wrongs sustain'd in France,
Either to get the town again or die:
And I, as sure as English Henry lives   80
And as his father here was conqueror,
As sure as in this late-betrayed town
Great Cœur-de-lion's heart was buried,
So sure I swear to get the town or die.

Bur. My vows are equal partners with thy vows.   85

Tal. But, ere we go, regard this dying prince,
The valiant Duke of Bedford.   Come, my lord,
We will bestow you in some better place,
Fitter for sickness and for crazy age.

Bed. Lord Talbot, do not so dishonour me.   90
Here will I sit before the walls of Rouen
And will be partner of your weal or woe.

Bur. Courageous Bedford, let us now persuade you.

Bed. Not to be gone from hence; for once I read
That stout Pendragon in his litter sick   95
Came to the field and vanquished his foes.
Methinks I should revive the soldiers' hearts,
Because I ever found them as myself.

Tal. Undaunted spirit in a dying breast!

Then be it so.   Heavens keep old Bedford safe!
And now no more ado, brave Burgundy,   101
But gather we our forces out of hand *forthwith*
And set upon our boasting enemy.

> *Exeunt [into the town all but Bedford and Attendants].*

An alarum: excursions.   Enter Sir John Fastolfe and a Captain.

Cap. Whither away, Sir John Fastolfe, in such haste?
Fast. Whither away! to save myself by flight.   105
   We are like to have the overthrow again.
Cap. What! will you fly, and leave Lord Talbot?
Fast.   Ay,
   All the Talbots in the world, to save my life.

> *Exit.*

Cap. Cowardly knight! ill fortune follow thee!

> *Exit [into the town].*

Retreat: excursions.   La Pucelle, Alençon, and Charles [enter from the town and] fly.

Bed. Now, quiet soul, depart when heaven please, 110
   For I have seen our enemies' overthrow.
   What is the trust or strength of foolish man?
   They that of late were daring with their scoffs
   Are glad and fain by flight to save themselves.

> *Bedford dies, and is carried in by two in his chair.*

An alarum. Re-enter Talbot, Burgundy, and the rest.

Tal. Lost, and recovered in a day again !   115
        This is a double honour, Burgundy ;
        Yet heavens have glory for this victory !
Bur. Warlike and martial Talbot, Burgundy
        Enshrines thee in his heart and there erects
        Thy noble deeds as valour's monuments.   120
Tal. Thanks, gentle duke.   But where is Pucelle now ?
        I think her old familiar is asleep.
        Now where's the Bastard's braves, and Charles his
        gleeks ?   *gibes dejected*
        What, all amort ?   Rouen hangs her head for grief
        That such a valiant company are fled.   125
        Now will we take some order in the town,
        Placing therein some expert officers,
        And then depart to Paris to the King,
        For there young Henry with his nobles lie.
Bur. What wills Lord Talbot pleaseth Burgundy.   130
Tal. But yet, before we go, let's not forget
        The noble Duke of Bedford late deceas'd,
        But see his exequies fulfill'd in Rouen.
        A braver soldier never couched lance,
        A gentler heart did never sway in court.   135
        But kings and mightiest potentates must die,
        For that's the end of human misery.
                                            Exeunt.

F

SCENE III

[The plains near Rouen.]

*Enter Charles, the Bastard of Orleans, Alençon, La
Pucelle [and forces].*

Puc. Dismay not, princes, at this accident,
Nor grieve that Rouen is so recovered.
Care is no cure, but rather corrosive, *fretting*
For things that are not to be remedi'd.
Let frantic Talbot triumph for a while   5
And like a peacock sweep along his tail;
We'll pull his plumes and take away his train,
If Dauphin and the rest will be but rul'd.
Char. We have been guided by thee hitherto
And of thy cunning had no diffidence. *distrust*   10
One sudden foil shall never breed distrust.
Bast. Search out thy wit for secret policies,
And we will make thee famous through the world.
Alen. We'll set thy statue in some holy place,
And have thee reverenc'd like a blessed saint.   15
Employ thee then, sweet virgin, for our good.
Puc. Then thus it must be; this doth Joan devise:
By fair persuasions mix'd with sug'red words
We will entice the Duke of Burgundy
To leave the Talbot and to follow us.   20
Char. Ay, marry, sweeting, if we could do that,
France were no place for Henry's warriors;

rooted out

Nor should that nation boast it so with us,
But be <u>extirp</u>ed from our provinces.

Alen. For ever should they be expuls'd from France 25
And not have title of an earldom here.

Puc. Your honours shall perceive how I will work
To bring this matter to the wished end.

> *Drum sounds afar off.*

Hark ! by the sound of drum you may perceive
Their powers are marching unto <u>Paris-ward.</u> *Paris* 30

Here sound an English march. [*Enter, and pass over
at a distance, Talbot and his forces.*]

There goes the Talbot, with his colours spread,
And all the troops of English after him.

French march. [*Enter the Duke of Burgundy and forces.*]

Now in the rearward comes the Duke and his.
Fortune in favour makes him lag behind.
Summon a parley ; we will talk with him.   35

> *Trumpets sound a parley.*

Char. A parley with the Duke of Burgundy !

Bur. Who craves a parley with the Burgundy ?

Puc. The princely Charles of France, thy countryman.

Bur. What say'st thou, Charles ? for I am marching
hence.

Char. Speak, Pucelle, and enchant him with thy
words.   40

Puc. Brave Burgundy, undoubted hope of France!
      Stay, let thy humble handmaid speak to thee.
Bur. Speak on ; but be not over-tedious.
Puc. Look on thy country, look on fertile France,
      And see the cities and the towns defac'd   45
      By wasting ruin of the cruel foe.
      As looks the mother on her lowly babe
      When death doth close his tender dying eyes,
      See, see the pining malady of France!
      Behold the wounds, the most unnatural wounds, 50
      Which thou thyself hast given her woeful breast.
      O, turn thy edged sword another way ;
      Strike those that hurt, and hurt not those that
          help.
      One drop of blood drawn from thy country's
          bosom
      Should grieve thee more than streams of foreign
          gore.   55
      Return thee therefore with a flood of tears,
      And wash away thy country's stained spots.
Bur. Either she hath bewitch'd me with her words,
      Or nature makes me suddenly relent.
Puc. Besides, all French and France exclaims on
          thee,   60
      Doubting thy birth and lawful progeny.
      Who join'st thou with but with a lordly nation
      That will not trust thee but for profit's sake?
      When Talbot hath set footing once in France

And fashion'd thee that instrument of ill,   65
Who then but English Henry will be lord
And thou be thrust out like a fugitive?
Call we to mind, and mark but this for proof,
Was not the Duke of Orleans thy foe?
And was he not in England prisoner?   70
But when they heard he was thine enemy,
They set him free without his ransom paid,
In spite of Burgundy and all his friends.
See, then, thou fight'st against thy countrymen
And join'st with them will be thy slaughter-
     men.   75
Come, come, return; return, thou wandering
     lord!
Charles and the rest will take thee in their
     arms.

Bur. I am vanquished. These haughty words of hers
Have batt'red me like roaring cannon-shot,
And made me almost yield upon my knees.   80
Forgive me, country, and sweet countrymen,
And, lords, accept this hearty kind embrace;
My forces and my power of men are yours.
So farewell, Talbot; I'll no longer trust thee.

Puc. [*Aside.*] Done like a Frenchman; turn, and
     turn again!   85

Char. Welcome, brave duke! thy friendship makes us
     fresh.

Bast. And doth beget new courage in our breasts.

Alen. Pucelle hath bravely play'd her part in this,
      And doth deserve a coronet of gold.

Char. Now let us on, my lords, and join our powers, 90
      And seek how we may prejudice the foe.

                        Exeunt.

SCENE IV

[Paris. The palace.]

Enter King Henry, Gloucester, Bishop of Winchester,
    York, Suffolk, Somerset, Warwick, Exeter [Vernon,
    Basset, and others]. To them with his Soldiers,
    Talbot.

Tal. My gracious prince, and honourable peers,
      Hearing of your arrival in this realm,
      I have a while given truce unto my wars
      To do my duty to my sovereign;
      In sign whereof, this arm, that hath reclaim'd   5
      To your obedience fifty fortresses,
      Twelve cities, and seven walled towns of strength,
      Beside five hundred prisoners of esteem,
      Lets fall his sword before your Highness' feet,
      And with submissive loyalty of heart   10
      Ascribes the glory of his conquest got
      First to my God and next unto your Grace.

                        [Kneels.]

King. Is this the Lord Talbot, uncle Gloucester,
      That hath so long been resident in France?

Glou. Yes, if it please your Majesty, my liege.   15

King. Welcome, brave captain and victorious lord !
　　When I was young, as yet I am not old,
　　I do remember how my father said
　　A stouter champion never handled sword.
　　Long since we were resolved of your truth,   20
　　Your faithful service, and your toil in war ;
　　Yet never have you tasted our reward,
　　Or been reguerdon'd with so much as thanks,
　　Because till now we never saw your face.
　　Therefore, stand up ; and, for these good
　　　　deserts,   25
　　We here create you Earl of Shrewsbury ;
　　And in our coronation take your place.
　　　　*Sennet.   Flourish.   Exeunt all but Vernon and
　　　　　　Basset.*

Ver. Now, sir, to you, that were so hot at sea,
　　Disgracing of these colours that I wear
　　In honour of my noble Lord of York :   30
　　Dar'st thou maintain the former words thou
　　　　spak'st ?

Bas. Yes, sir ; as well as you dare patronage
　　The envious barking of your saucy tongue
　　Against my lord the Duke of Somerset.

Ver. Sirrah, thy lord I honour as he is.   35

Bas. Why, what is he ? As good a man as York.

Ver. Hark ye, not so ; in witness, take ye that.
　　　　　　　　　　Strikes him.

Bas. Villain, thou know'st the law of arms is such
    That whoso draws a sword, 'tis present death,
    Or else this blow should broach thy dearest
      blood.   40
    But I'll unto his Majesty, and crave
    I may have liberty to venge this wrong;
    When thou shalt see I'll meet thee to thy cost.
Ver. Well, miscreant, I'll be there as soon as you;
    And, after, meet you sooner than you would.   45
                                    Exeunt.

ACT FOURTH

SCENE I

[Paris. A hall of state.]

*Enter King Henry, Gloucester, Bishop of Winchester,
York, Suffolk, Somerset, Warwick, Talbot, Exeter,
the Governor of Paris [and others].*

Glou. Lord Bishop, set the crown upon his head.
Win. God save King Henry, of that name the sixth !
Glou. Now, governor of Paris, take your oath,
    That you elect no other king but him ;

                  [Governor kneels.]

    Esteem none friends but such as are his friends, 5
    And none your foes but such as shall pretend
    Malicious practices against his state.
    This shall ye do, so help you righteous God !

                  [Exeunt Governor, etc.]

      Enter Sir John Fastolfe.

Fast. My gracious sovereign, as I rode from Calais,
    To haste unto your coronation,   10
    A letter was deliver'd to my hands,
    Writ to your Grace from the Duke of Burgundy.

Tal. Shame to the Duke of Burgundy and thee!
I vow'd, base knight, when I did meet thee next,
To tear the Garter from thy craven's leg, 15
[Plucking it off.]
Which I have done, because unworthily
Thou wast installed in that high degree.
Pardon me, princely Henry, and the rest.
This dastard, at the battle of Poictiers,
When but in all I was six thousand strong 20
And that the French were almost ten to one,
Before we met or that a stroke was given,
Like to a trusty squire did run away;
In which assault we lost twelve hundred men;
Myself and divers gentlemen beside 25
Were there surpris'd and taken prisoners.
Then judge, great lords, if I have done amiss;
Or whether that such cowards ought to wear
This ornament of knighthood, yea or no.

Glou. To say the truth, this fact was infamous 30
And ill beseeming any common man,
Much more a knight, a captain, and a leader.

Tal. When first this order was ordain'd, my lords,
Knights of the Garter were of noble birth,
Valiant and virtuous, full of haughty courage, 35
Such as were grown to credit by the wars;
Not fearing death, nor shrinking for distress,
But always resolute in most extremes.
He then that is not furnish'd in this sort

Doth but usurp the sacred name of knight,   40
Profaning this most honourable order,
And should, if I were worthy to be judge,
Be quite degraded, like a hedge-born swain
That doth presume to boast of gentle blood.

King. Stain to thy countrymen, thou hear'st thy
     doom !   45
Be packing, therefore, thou that wast a knight ;
Henceforth we banish thee, on pain of death.

                     [*Exit Fastolfe.*]

And now, my Lord Protector, view the letter
Sent from our uncle Duke of Burgundy.

Glou. What means his Grace, that he hath chang'd
     his style ?   50
No more but, plain and bluntly, "To the King !"
Hath he forgot he is his sovereign ?
Or doth this churlish superscription
Pretend some alteration in good will ?
What's here ?

[*Reads.*]   "I have, upon especial cause,   55
Mov'd with compassion of my country's wreck,
Together with the pitiful complaints
Of such as your oppression feeds upon,
Forsaken your pernicious faction
And join'd with Charles, the rightful King of
     France."   60
O monstrous treachery ! can this be so,
That in alliance, amity, and oaths,

There should be found such false dissembling
    guile?

King. What! doth my uncle Burgundy revolt?

Glou. He doth, my lord, and is become your foe.   65

King. Is that the worst this letter doth contain?

Glou. It is the worst, and all, my lord, he writes.

King. Why, then, Lord Talbot there shall talk with him
    And give him chastisement for this abuse.

    How say you, my lord? Are you not content? 70

Tal. Content, my liege? Yes. But that I am pre-
    vented,

    I should have begg'd I might have been employ'd.

King. Then gather strength and march unto him
    straight.

    Let him perceive how ill we brook his treason,
    And what offence it is to flout his friends.   75

Tal. I go, my lord, in heart desiring still
    You may behold confusion of your foes.   *Exit.*

Enter Vernon and Basset.

Ver. Grant me the combat, gracious sovereign.

Bas. And me, my lord, grant me the combat too.

York. This is my servant; hear him, noble prince.   80

Som. And this is mine; sweet Henry, favour him.

K. Hen. Be patient, lords; and give them leave to
    speak.

    Say, gentlemen, what makes you thus exclaim?
    And wherefore crave you combat? or with whom?

Ver. With him, my lord; for he hath done me
     wrong.   85

Bas. And I with him; for he hath done me wrong.

K. Hen. What is that wrong whereof you both com-
     plain?

     First let me know, and then I'll answer you.

Bas. Crossing the sea from England into France,

     This fellow here, with envious carping tongue,   90

     Upbraided me about the rose I wear,

     Saying the sanguine colour of the leaves

     Did represent my master's blushing cheeks,

     When stubbornly he did repugn the truth

     About a certain question in the law   95

     Argued betwixt the Duke of York and him;

     With other vile and ignominious terms;

     In confutation of which rude reproach

     And in defence of my lord's worthiness,

     I crave the benefit of law of arms.   100

Ver. And that is my petition, noble lord.

     For though he seem with forged quaint conceit

     To set a gloss upon his bold intent,

     Yet know, my lord, I was provok'd by him;

     And he first took exceptions at this badge,   105

     Pronouncing that the paleness of this flower

     Bewray'd the faintness of my master's heart.

York. Will not this malice, Somerset, be left?

Som. Your private grudge, my Lord of York, will out,

     Though ne'er so cunningly you smother it.   110

K. Hen. Good Lord, what madness rules in brainsick
      men,
    When for so slight and frivolous a cause
    Such factious emulations shall arise!
    Good cousins both, of York and Somerset,
    Quiet yourselves, I pray, and be at peace.   115

York. Let this dissension first be tried by fight,
    And then your Highness shall command a peace.

Som. The quarrel toucheth none but us alone;
    Betwixt ourselves let us decide it then.

York. There is my pledge; accept it, Somerset.   120

Ver. Nay, let it rest where it began at first.

Bas. Confirm it so, mine honourable lord.

Glou. Confirm it so! Confounded be your strife!
    And perish ye, with your audacious prate!
    Presumptuous vassals, are you not asham'd   125
    With this immodest clamorous outrage
    To trouble and disturb the King and us?
    And you, my lords, methinks you do not well
    To bear with their perverse objections;
    Much less to take occasion from their mouths   130
    To raise a mutiny betwixt yourselves.
    Let me persuade you take a better course.

Exe. It grieves his Highness. Good my lords, be
      friends.

K. Hen. Come hither, you that would be combatants.
    Henceforth I charge you, as you love our fa-
      vour,   135

Quite to forget this quarrel and the cause.
And you, my lords, remember where we are;
In France, amongst a fickle, wavering nation.
If they perceive dissension in our looks
And that within ourselves we disagree,   140
How will their grudging stomachs be provok'd
To wilful disobedience, and rebel !
Beside, what infamy will there arise,
When foreign princes shall be certified
That for a toy, a thing of no regard,   145
King Henry's peers and chief nobility
Destroy'd themselves, and lost the realm of
     France !
O, think upon the conquest of my father,
My tender years, and let us not forgo
That for a trifle that was bought with blood ! 150
Let me be umpire in this doubtful strife.
I see no reason, if I wear this rose,
                    [*Putting on a red rose.*]
That any one should therefore be suspicious
I more incline to Somerset than York.
Both are my kinsmen, and I love them both.   155
As well they may upbraid me with my crown,
Because, forsooth, the King of Scots is crown'd.
But your discretions better can persuade
Than I am able to instruct or teach ;
And therefore, as we hither came in peace,   160
So let us still continue peace and love.

Cousin of York, we institute your Grace
To be our regent in these parts of France;
And, good my Lord of Somerset, unite
Your troops of horsemen with his bands of foot; 165
And, like true subjects, sons of your progenitors,
Go cheerfully together and digest
Your angry choler on your enemies.
Ourself, my Lord Protector, and the rest
After some respite will return to Calais;   170
From thence to England; where I hope ere long
To be presented, by your victories,
With Charles, Alençon, and that traitorous rout.
     Exeunt all but York, Warwick, Exeter and
        Vernon.

War. My Lord of York, I promise you, the King
    Prettily, methought, did play the orator.   175
York. And so he did; but yet I like it not,
    In that he wears the badge of Somerset.
War. Tush, that was but his fancy, blame him not.
    I dare presume, sweet prince, he thought no harm.
York. An if I wist he did, — but let it rest;   180
    Other affairs must now be managed.
            Flourish.   Exeunt all but Exeter.
Exe. Well didst thou, Richard, to suppress thy voice;
    For, had the passions of thy heart burst out,
    I fear we should have seen decipher'd there
    More rancorous spite, more furious raging
       broils,   185

Than yet can be imagin'd or suppos'd.
But howsoe'er, no simple man that sees
This jarring discord of nobility,
This shouldering of each other in the court,
This factious bandying of their favourites,   190
But that it doth presage some ill event.
'Tis much when sceptres are in children's hands;
But more when envy breeds unkind division.
There comes the ruin, there begins confusion.

Exit.

SCENE II

Before Bourdeaux.

Enter Talbot, with trump and drum.

Tal. Go to the gates of Bourdeaux, trumpeter;
   Summon their general unto the wall.

Trumpet sounds.   Enter General [and others,] aloft.

English John Talbot, captains, calls you forth,
Servant in arms to Harry King of England,
And thus he would: Open your city gates;   5
Be humble to us; call my sovereign yours,
And do him homage as obedient subjects;
And I'll withdraw me and my bloody power.
But, if you frown upon this proffer'd peace,
You tempt the fury of my three attendants,   10
Lean famine, quartering steel, and climbing fire;

G

Who in a moment even with the earth
Shall lay your stately and air-braving towers,
If you forsake the offer of their love.

Gen. Thou ominous and fearful owl of death, 15
Our nation's terror and their bloody scourge!
The period of thy tyranny approacheth.
On us thou canst not enter but by death;
For, I protest, we are well fortified
And strong enough to issue out and fight. 20
If thou retire, the Dauphin, well appointed,
Stands with the snares of war to tangle thee.
On either hand thee there are squadrons pitch'd,
To wall thee from the liberty of flight;
And no way canst thou turn thee for redress 25
But death doth front thee with apparent spoil,
And pale destruction meets thee in the face.
Ten thousand French have ta'en the sacrament
To rive their dangerous artillery
Upon no Christian soul but English Talbot. 30
Lo, there thou stand'st, a breathing valiant man,
Of an invincible unconquer'd spirit!
This is the latest glory of thy praise
That I, thy enemy, due thee withal;
For ere the glass, that now begins to run, 35
Finish the process of his sandy hour,
These eyes, that see thee now well coloured,
Shall see thee withered, bloody, pale, and dead.
Drum afar off.

Hark! hark! the Dauphin's drum, a warning bell,
Sings heavy music to thy timorous soul ; 40
And mine shall ring thy dire departure out.

Exeunt [General, etc.].

Tal. He fables not ; I hear the enemy.
Out, some light horsemen, and peruse their wings.
O, negligent and heedless discipline !
How are we park'd and bounded in a pale, 45
A little herd of England's timorous deer,
Maz'd with a yelping kennel of French curs !
If we be English deer, be then in blood ;
Not rascal-like, to fall down with a pinch,
But rather, moody-mad and desperate stags, 50
Turn on the bloody hounds with heads of steel
And make the cowards stand aloof at bay.
Sell every man his life as dear as mine,
And they shall find dear deer of us, my friends.
God and Saint George, Talbot and England's
right, 55
Prosper our colours in this dangerous fight !

[Exeunt.]

SCENE III

[Plains in Gascony.]

*Enter York, with trumpet and many Soldiers: to him
a Messenger.*

York. Are not the speedy scouts return'd again,
That dogg'd the mighty army of the Dauphin ?

Mess. They are return'd, my lord, and give it out
    That he is march'd to Bourdeaux with his power,
    To fight with Talbot. As he march'd along,   5
    By your espials were discovered
    Two mightier troops than that the Dauphin led,
    Which join'd with him and made their march for
        Bourdeaux.
York. A plague upon that villain Somerset,
    That thus delays my promised supply   10
    Of horsemen, that were levied for this siege !
    Renowned Talbot doth expect my aid,
    And I am louted by a traitor villain
    And cannot help the noble chevalier.
    God comfort him in this necessity !   15
    If he miscarry, farewell wars in France !

Enter another Messenger [Sir William Lucy].

[*Lucy.*] Thou princely leader of our English strength,
    Never so needful on the earth of France,
    Spur to the rescue of the noble Talbot,
    Who now is girdled with a waist of iron   20
    And hemm'd about with grim destruction.
    To Bourdeaux, warlike duke ! to Bourdeaux,
        York !
    Else, farewell Talbot, France, and England's
        honour !
York. O God, that Somerset, who in proud heart
    Doth stop my cornets, were in Talbot's place ! 25

So should we save a valiant gentleman
By forfeiting a traitor and a coward.
Mad ire and wrathful fury makes me weep,
That thus we die, while remiss traitors sleep.

[*Lucy.*] O, send some succour to the distress'd lord ! 30

York. He dies, we lose ; I break my warlike word ;
We mourn, France smiles ; we lose, they daily get ;
All long of this vile traitor Somerset.

[*Lucy.*] Then God take mercy on brave Talbot's soul,
And on his son young John, who two hours since 35
I met in travel toward his warlike father !
This seven years did not Talbot see his son,
And now they meet where both their lives are done.

York. Alas, what joy shall noble Talbot have
To bid his young son welcome to his grave ?   40
Away ! vexation almost stops my breath,
That sund'red friends greet in the hour of death.
Lucy, farewell ; no more my fortune can,
But curse the cause I cannot aid the man.
Maine, Blois, Poictiers, and Tours, are won
    away,   45
Long all of this Somerset and his delay.

Exit [*with his soldiers*].

[*Lucy.*] Thus, while the vulture of sedition
Feeds in the bosom of such great commanders,
Sleeping neglection doth betray to loss
The conquest of our scarce cold conqueror,   50
That ever living man of memory,

Man of ever living memory,

Henry the Fifth.   Whiles they each other cross,
Lives, honours, lands, and all hurry to loss.

                               [Exit.]

SCENE IV

[Other plains in Gascony.]

*Enter Somerset, with his army [a Captain of Talbot's
with him].*

Som.   It is too late ; I cannot send them now.
This expedition was by York and Talbot
Too rashly plotted.   All our general force
Might with a sally of the very town
Be buckled with.   The over-daring Talbot   5
Hath sullied all his gloss of former honour
By this unheedful, desperate, wild adventure.
York set him on to fight and die in shame,
That, Talbot dead, great York might bear the name.
Cap.   Here is Sir William Lucy, who with me   10
Set from our o'ermatch'd forces forth for aid.

Enter Sir William Lucy.

Som.   How now, Sir William ! whither were you sent ?
Lucy.   Whither, my lord ?   From bought and sold
          Lord Talbot ;
Who, ring'd about with bold adversity,
Cries out for noble York and Somerset   15
To beat assailing death from his weak legions ;

And whiles the honourable captain there
Drops bloody sweat from his war-wearied limbs,
And, in advantage ling'ring, looks for rescue,
You, his false hopes, the trust of England's
    honour,   20
Keep off aloof with worthless emulation.
Let not your private discord keep away
The levied succours that should lend him aid,
While he, renowned noble gentleman,
Yield up his life unto a world of odds.   25
Orleans the Bastard, Charles, Burgundy,
Alençon, Reignier, compass him about,
And Talbot perisheth by your default.

Som. York set him on ; York should have sent him aid.

Lucy. And York as fast upon your Grace exclaims, 30
Swearing that you withhold his levied host,
Collected for this expedition.

Som. York lies ; he might have sent and had the
    horse.
I owe him little duty, and less love ;
And take foul scorn to fawn on him by sending. 35

Lucy. The fraud of England, not the force of France,
Hath now entrapp'd the noble-minded Talbot.
Never to England shall he bear his life,
But dies, betray'd to fortune by your strife.

Som. Come, go ; I will dispatch the horsemen
    straight.   40
Within six hours they will be at his aid.

Lucy. Too late comes rescue.   He is ta'en or slain ;
      For fly he could not, if he would have fled ;
      And fly would Talbot never, though he might.
Som. If he be dead, brave Talbot, then adieu !   45
Lucy. His fame lives in the world, his shame in you.
                            Exeunt.

SCENE V

[The English camp near Bourdeaux.]

· *Enter Talbot and [John] his son.*

Tal. O young John Talbot !   I did send for thee
      To tutor thee in stratagems of war,
      That Talbot's name might be in thee reviv'd
      When sapless age and weak unable limbs
      Should bring thy father to his drooping chair.   5
      But, O malignant and ill-boding stars !
      Now thou art come unto a feast of death,
      A terrible and unavoided danger.
      Therefore, dear boy, mount on my swiftest horse ;
      And I'll direct thee how thou shalt escape   10
      By sudden flight.   Come, dally not, be gone.
John. Is my name Talbot ? and am I your son ?
      And shall I fly ?   O, if you love my mother,
      Dishonour not her honourable name,
      To make a bastard and a slave of me !   15
      The world will say, he is not Talbot's blood,
      That basely fled when noble Talbot stood.

Tal. Fly, to revenge my death, if I be slain.

John. He that flies so will ne'er return again.

Tal. If we both stay, we both are sure to die.　20

John. Then let me stay; and, father, do you fly.
　　Your loss is great, so your regard should be;
　　My worth unknown, no loss is known in me.
　　Upon my death the French can little boast;
　　In yours they will, in you all hopes are lost.　25
　　Flight cannot stain the honour you have won,
　　But mine it will, that no exploit have done.
　　You fled for vantage, every one will swear;
　　But, if I bow, they'll say it was for fear.
　　There is no hope that ever I will stay,　30
　　If the first hour I shrink and run away.
　　Here on my knee I beg mortality,
　　Rather than life preserv'd with infamy.

Tal. Shall all thy mother's hopes lie in one tomb?

John. Ay, rather than I'll shame my mother's womb. 35

Tal. Upon my blessing, I command thee go.

John. To fight I will, but not to fly the foe.

Tal. Part of thy father may be sav'd in thee.

John. No part of him but will be shame in me.

Tal. Thou never hadst renown, nor canst not lose
　　it.　40

John. Yes, your renowned name. Shall flight abuse
　　it?

Tal. Thy father's charge shall clear thee from that
　　stain.

John. You cannot witness for me, being slain.
      If death be so apparent, then both fly.
Tal. And leave my followers here to fight and die ?   45
      My age was never tainted with such shame.
John. And shall my youth be guilty of such blame ?
      No more can I be severed from your side,
      Than can yourself yourself in twain divide.
      Stay, go, do what you will, the like do I ;   50
      For live I will not, if my father die.
Tal. Then here I take my leave of thee, fair son,
      Born to eclipse thy life this afternoon.
      Come, side by side together live and die ;
      And soul with soul from France to heaven fly.   55

                                    Exeunt.

SCENE VI

[A field of battle.]

*Alarum: excursions, wherein John Talbot is hemmed
      about, and Talbot rescues him.*

Tal. Saint George and victory ! fight, soldiers, fight !
      The Regent hath with Talbot broke his word
      And left us to the rage of France his sword.
      Where is John Talbot ? Pause, and take thy
            breath ;
      I gave thee life and rescu'd thee from death.   5
John. O, twice my father, twice am I thy son !

The life thou gav'st me first was lost and done,
Till with thy warlike sword, despite of fate,
To my determin'd time thou gav'st new date.

Tal. When from the Dauphin's crest thy sword struck
      fire,   10
It warm'd thy father's heart with proud desire
Of bold-fac'd victory.   Then leaden age,
Quicken'd with youthful spleen and warlike rage,
Beat down Alençon, Orleans, Burgundy,
And from the pride of Gallia rescued thee.   15
The ireful bastard Orleans, that drew blood
From thee, my boy, and had the maidenhood
Of thy first fight, I soon encountered,
And interchanging blows I quickly shed
Some of his bastard blood; and in disgrace   20
Bespoke him thus: "Contaminated, base,
And misbegotten blood I spill of thine,
Mean and right poor, for that pure blood of mine
Which thou didst force from Talbot, my brave
      boy."
Here, purposing the Bastard to destroy,   25
Came in strong rescue.   Speak, thy father's care,
Art thou not weary, John?   How dost thou fare?
Wilt thou yet leave the battle, boy, and fly,
Now thou art seal'd the son of chivalry?
Fly, to revenge my death when I am dead;   30
The help of one stands me in little stead.
O, too much folly is it, well I wot,

To hazard all our lives in one small boat !
If I to-day die not with Frenchmen's rage,
To-morrow I shall die with mickle age.   35
By me they nothing gain an if I stay ;
'Tis but the short'ning of my life one day.
In thee thy mother dies, our household's name,
My death's revenge, thy youth, and England's
    fame.
All these and more we hazard by thy stay ;   40
All these are sav'd if thou wilt fly away.

John. The sword of Orleans hath not made me smart ;
These words of yours draw life-blood from my
    heart.
On that advantage, bought with such a shame,
To save a paltry life and slay bright fame,   45
Before young Talbot from old Talbot fly,
The coward horse that bears me fall and die !
And like me to the peasant boys of France,
To be shame's scorn and subject of mischance !
Surely, by all the glory you have won,   50
An if I fly, I am not Talbot's son.
Then talk no more of flight, it is no boot ;
If son to Talbot, die at Talbot's foot.

Tal. Then follow thou thy desperate sire of Crete,
Thou Icarus. Thy life to me is sweet.   55
If thou wilt fight, fight by thy father's side ;
And, commendable prov'd, let's die in pride.

                                 Exeunt.

SCENE VII

[Another part of the field.]

Alarum: excursions. Enter old Talbot led [by a Servant].

Tal. Where is my other life? mine own is gone.
    O, where's young Talbot? where is valiant John?
    Triumphant Death, smear'd with captivity,
    Young Talbot's valour makes me smile at thee.
    When he perceiv'd me sink and on my knee,   5
    His bloody sword he brandish'd over me,
    And, like a hungry lion, did commence
    Rough deeds of rage and stern impatience;
    But when my angry guardant stood alone,
    Tend'ring my ruin and assail'd of none,   10
    Dizzy-ey'd fury and great rage of heart
    Suddenly made him from my side to start
    Into the clust'ring battle of the French;
    And in that sea of blood my boy did drench
    His over-mounting spirit, and there died,   15
    My Icarus, my blossom, in his pride.

Enter [Soldiers,] with the body of John Talbot.

Serv. O my dear lord, lo, where your son is borne!
Tal. Thou antic Death, which laugh'st us here to
        scorn,
    Anon, from thy insulting tyranny,

Coupled in bonds of perpetuity,   20
Two Talbots, winged through the lither sky,
In thy despite shall scape mortality.
O thou, whose wounds become hard-favoured
    Death,
Speak to thy father ere thou yield thy breath!
Brave Death by speaking, whether he will or no; 25
Imagine him a Frenchman and thy foe.
Poor boy! he smiles, methinks, as who should
    say,
Had Death been French, then Death had died
    to-day.
Come, come, and lay him in his father's arms.
My spirit can no longer bear these harms.   30
Soldiers, adieu! I have what I would have,
Now my old arms are young John Talbot's
    grave.   *Dies.*

*Enter Charles, Alençon, Burgundy, Bastard, La Pucelle
    [and forces].*

Char. Had York and Somerset brought rescue in,
    We should have found a bloody day of this.
Bast. How the young whelp of Talbot's, raging
    wood,   35
    Did flesh his puny sword in Frenchmen's blood!
Puc. Once I encount'red him, and thus I said:
    "Thou maiden youth, be vanquish'd by a maid!"
    But, with a proud majestical high scorn,

He answer'd thus: "Young Talbot was not
    born   40
To be the pillage of a *wanton* giglot wench."
So, rushing in the bowels of the French,
He left me proudly, as unworthy fight.

Bur. Doubtless he would have made a noble knight.
    See, where he lies inhearsed in the arms   45
    Of the most bloody nurser of his harms!

Bast. Hew them to pieces, hack their bones asunder,
    Whose life was England's glory, Gallia's wonder.

Char. O, no, forbear! for that which we have fled
    During the life, let us not wrong it dead.   50

*Enter Sir William Lucy [attended; Herald of the French
preceding].*

Lucy. Herald, conduct me to the Dauphin's tent
    To know who hath obtain'd the glory of the day.

Char. On what submissive message art thou sent?

Lucy. Submission, Dauphin! 'tis a mere French word;
    We English warriors wot not what it means.   55
    I come to know what prisoners thou hast ta'en
    And to survey the bodies of the dead.

Char. For prisoners ask'st thou? Hell our prison is.
    But tell me whom thou seek'st.

Lucy. But where's the great Alcides of the field,   60
    Valiant Lord Talbot, Earl of Shrewsbury,
    Created, for his rare success in arms,
    Great Earl of Washford, Waterford, and Valence;

Lord Talbot of Goodrig and Urchinfield,
Lord Strange of Blackmere, Lord Verdun of
    Alton,   65
Lord Cromwell of Wingfield, Lord Furnival of
    Sheffield,
The thrice-victorious Lord of Falconbridge ;
Knight of the noble Order of Saint George,
Worthy Saint Michael, and the Golden Fleece ;
Great Marshal to Henry the Sixth   70
Of all his wars within the realm of France ?

Puc. Here is a silly stately style indeed !
The Turk, that two and fifty kingdoms hath,
Writes not so tedious a style as this.
Him that thou magnifi'st with all these titles   75
Stinking and fly-blown lies here at our feet.

Lucy. Is Talbot slain, the Frenchmen's only scourge,
Your kingdom's terror and black Nemesis ?
O, were mine eye-balls into bullets turn'd,
That I in rage might shoot them at your faces ! 80
O, that I could but call these dead to life !
It were enough to fright the realm of France.
Were but his picture left amongst you here,
It would amaze the proudest of you all.
Give me their bodies, that I may bear them
    hence   85
And give them burial as beseems their worth.

Puc. I think this upstart is old Talbot's ghost,
He speaks with such a proud commanding spirit.

For God's sake, let him have him.   To keep them here,

They would but stink, and putrefy the air.   90

Char.   Go, take their bodies hence.

Lucy.   I'll bear them hence ; but from their ashes shall be rear'd

A phœnix that shall make all France afeard.

Char.   So we be rid of them, do with them what thou wilt.

And now to Paris, in this conquering vein ;   95

All will be ours, now bloody Talbot's slain.

                                             Exeunt.

ACT FIFTH

SCENE I

[London. The palace.]

Sennet. Enter King, Gloucester, and Exeter.

King. Have you perus'd the letters from the Pope,
    The Emperor, and the Earl of Armagnac?
Glou. I have, my lord; and their intent is this:
    They humbly sue unto your excellence
    To have a godly peace concluded of   5
    Between the realms of England and of France.
King. How doth your Grace affect their motion?
Glou. Well, my good lord; and as the only means
    To stop effusion of our Christian blood
    And stablish quietness on every side.   10
King. Ay, marry, uncle; for I always thought
    It was both impious and unnatural
    That such immanity and bloody strife
    Should reign among professors of one faith.
Glou. Beside, my lord, the sooner to effect   15
    And surer bind this knot of amity,
    The Earl of Armagnac, near knit to Charles,
    A man of great authority in France,
    Proffers his only daughter to your Grace
    In marriage, with a large and sumptuous dowry.

King. Marriage, uncle ! Alas, my years are young ! 21
     And fitter is my study and my books
     Than wanton dalliance with a paramour.
     Yet call the ambassadors ; and, as you please,
     So let them have their answers every one.   25
     I shall be well content with any choice
     Tends to God's glory and my country's weal.

Enter Winchester [in Cardinal's habit, a Legate, and two]
                 Ambassadors.

Exe. What ! is my Lord of Winchester install'd,
     And call'd unto a cardinal's degree ?
     Then I perceive that will be verified   30
     Henry the Fifth did sometime prophesy,
     "If once he come to be a cardinal,
     He'll make his cap co-equal with the crown."
King. My lords ambassadors, your several suits
     Have been consider'd and debated on.   35
     Your purpose is both good and reasonable ;
     And therefore are we certainly resolv'd
     To draw conditions of a friendly peace ;
     Which by my Lord of Winchester we mean
     Shall be transported presently to France.   40
Glou. And for the proffer of my lord your master,
     I have inform'd his Highness so at large ;
     As liking of the lady's virtuous gifts,
     Her beauty, and the value of her dower,
     He doth intend she shall be England's queen.   45

King. [*To the Amb.*] In argument and proof of which
  contract,
  Bear her this jewel, pledge of my affection.
  And so, my Lord Protector, see them guarded
  And safely brought to Dover; where inshipp'd
  Commit them to the fortune of the sea.   50
     Exeunt [*all but Winchester and Legate*].
Win. Stay, my lord legate; you shall first receive
  The sum of money which I promised
  Should be delivered to his Holiness
  For clothing me in these grave ornaments.
Leg. I will attend upon your lordship's leisure. 55
Win. [*Aside.*] Now Winchester will not submit, I trow,
  Or be inferior to the proudest peer.
  Humphrey of Gloucester, thou shalt well perceive
  That, neither in birth or for authority,
  The Bishop will be overborne by thee.   60
  I'll either make thee stoop and bend thy knee,
  Or sack this country with a mutiny.   *Exeunt.*

SCENE II

[*France.   Plains in Anjou.*]

*Enter Charles, Burgundy, Alençon, Bastard, Reignier,
  La Pucelle* [*and forces*].

Char. These news, my lords, may cheer our drooping
  spirits.

'Tis said the stout Parisians do revolt
And turn again unto the warlike French.

Alen. Then march to Paris, royal Charles of France,
And keep not back your powers in dalliance.   5

Puc. Peace be amongst them, if they turn to us;
Else, ruin combat with their palaces!

Enter Scout.

Scout. Success unto our valiant general,
And happiness to his accomplices!

Char. What tidings send our scouts? I prithee, speak. 10

Scout. The English army, that divided was
Into two parties, is now conjoin'd in one,
And means to give you battle presently.

Char. Somewhat too sudden, sirs, the warning is;
But we will presently provide for them.   15

Bur. I trust the ghost of Talbot is not there.
Now he is gone, my lord, you need not fear.

Puc. Of all base passions, fear is most accurs'd.
Command the conquest, Charles, it shall be thine.
Let Henry fret and all the world repine.   20

Char. Then on, my lords; and France be fortunate!

Exeunt.

SCENE III

[Before Angiers.]

Alarum. Excursions. Enter La Pucelle.

Puc. The Regent conquers, and the Frenchmen fly.
Now help, ye charming spells and periapts; *charms*

And ye choice spirits that admonish me
And give me signs of future accidents.

Thunder.

You speedy helpers, that are substitutes   5
Under the lordly monarch of the north,
Appear and aid me in this enterprise.

Enter Fiends.

This speedy and quick appearance argues proof
Of your accustom'd diligence to me.
Now, ye familiar spirits, that are cull'd   10
Out of the powerful regions under earth,
Help me this once, that France may get the field.

They walk, and speak not.

O, hold me not with silence over-long !
Where I was wont to feed you with my blood,
I'll lop a member off and give it you   15
In earnest of a further benefit,
So you do condescend to help me now.

They hang their heads.

No hope to have redress ?   My body shall
Pay recompense, if you will grant my suit.

They shake their heads.

Cannot my body nor blood-sacrifice   20
Entreat you to your wonted furtherance ?
Then take my soul, my body, soul, and all,
Before that England give the French the foil.

They depart.

See, they forsake me!   Now the time is come
That France must vail her lofty-plumed crest   25
And let her head fall into England's lap.
My ancient incantations are too weak,
And hell too strong for me to buckle with.
Now, France, thy glory droopeth to the dust.

Exit.

*Excursions. Enter Burgundy and York fighting hand
    to hand. The French fly. [La Pucelle is brought
    in captive.]*

York. Damsel of France, I think I have you fast.   30
    Unchain your spirits now with spelling charms
    And try if they can gain your liberty.
    A goodly prize, fit for the devil's grace!
    See, how the ugly wench doth bend her brows,
    As if with Circe she would change my shape!   35
Puc. Chang'd to a worser shape thou canst not be.
York. O, Charles the Dauphin is a proper man;
    No shape but his can please your dainty eye.
Puc. A plaguing mischief light on Charles and thee!
    And may ye both be suddenly surpris'd   40
    By bloody hands, in sleeping on your beds!
York. Fell banning hag, enchantress, hold thy tongue!
Puc. I prithee, give me leave to curse a while.
York. Curse, miscreant, when thou com'st to the
    stake.   *Exeunt.*

Alarum.   Enter Suffolk, with Margaret in his hand.

Suf. Be what thou wilt, thou art my prisoner.

Gazes on her.

    O fairest beauty, do not fear nor fly,   46
    For I will touch thee but with reverent hands.
    I kiss these fingers for eternal peace,
    And lay them gently on thy tender side.
    Who art thou? say, that I may honour thee.   50
Mar. Margaret my name, and daughter to a king,
    The King of Naples, whosoe'er thou art.
Suf. An earl I am, and Suffolk am I call'd.
    Be not offended, nature's miracle,
    Thou art allotted to be ta'en by me;   55
    So doth the swan her downy cygnets save,
    Keeping them prisoner underneath her wings.
    Yet, if this servile usage once offend,
    Go and be free again as Suffolk's friend.

She is going.

    O, stay! [*Aside.*] I have no power to let her
        pass;   60
    My hand would free her, but my heart says no.
    As plays the sun upon the glassy streams,
    Twinkling another counterfeited beam,
    So seems this gorgeous beauty to mine eyes.
    Fain would I woo her, yet I dare not speak.   65
    I'll call for pen and ink, and write my mind.
    Fie, De la Pole! disable not thyself.

Hast not a tongue?   Is she not here?
Wilt thou be daunted at a woman's sight?
Ay, beauty's princely majesty is such,   70
Confounds the tongue and makes the senses rough,   *makes dull or ruffles the senses*

Mar. Say, Earl of Suffolk — if thy name be so —
What ransom must I pay before I pass?
For I perceive I am thy prisoner.

Suf. [*Aside.*] How canst thou tell she will deny thy
      suit,   75
Before thou make a trial of her love?

Mar. Why speak'st thou not?   What ransom must I
      pay?

Suf. [*Aside.*] She's beautiful and therefore to be woo'd;
She is a woman, therefore to be won.

Mar. Wilt thou accept of ransom? yea, or no.   80

Suf. [*Aside.*] Fond man, remember that thou hast a
      wife;
Then how can Margaret be thy paramour?

Mar. I were best to leave him, for he will not hear.

Suf. [*Aside.*] There all is marr'd; there lies a cooling
      card.

Mar. He talks at random; sure, the man is mad.   85

Suf. [*Aside.*] And yet a dispensation may be had.

Mar. And yet I would that you would answer me.

Suf. [*Aside.*] I'll win this Lady Margaret. For
      whom?
Why, for my king. Tush, that's a wooden thing!   *mad*

Mar. He talks of wood; it is some carpenter.   90

Suf. [*Aside.*] Yet so my fancy may be satisfied,
And peace established between these realms.
But there remains a scruple in that too ;
For though her father be the King of Naples,
Duke of Anjou and Maine, yet is he poor,   95
And our nobility will scorn the match.

Mar. Hear ye, captain ? Are you not at leisure ?

Suf. [*Aside.*] It shall be so, disdain they ne'er so much.
Henry is youthful and will quickly yield.
Madam, I have a secret to reveal.   100

Mar. [*Aside.*] What though I be enthrall'd ? He
seems a knight,
And will not any way dishonour me.

Suf. Lady, vouchsafe to listen what I say.

Mar. [*Aside.*] Perhaps I shall be rescu'd by the French ;
And then I need not crave his courtesy.   105

Suf. Sweet madam, give me hearing in a cause —

Mar. [*Aside.*] Tush, women have been captivate ere
now.

Suf. Lady, wherefore talk you so ?

Mar. I cry you mercy, 'tis but *quid* for *quo*.

Suf. Say, gentle princess, would you not suppose   110
Your bondage happy, to be made a queen ?

Mar. To be a queen in bondage is more vile
Than is a slave in base servility ;
For princes should be free.

Suf.   And so shall you,
If happy England's royal king be free.   115

Mar. Why, what concerns his freedom unto me?

Suf. I'll undertake to make thee Henry's queen,
     To put a golden sceptre in thy hand
     And set a precious crown upon thy head,
     If thou wilt condescend to be my —

Mar.   What?   120

Suf. His love.

Mar. I am unworthy to be Henry's wife.

Suf. No, gentle madam; I unworthy am
     To woo so fair a dame to be his wife
     And have no portion in the choice myself.   125
     How say you, madam, are ye so content?

Mar. An if my father please, I am content.

Suf. Then call our captains and our colours forth.
     And, madam, at your father's castle walls
     We'll crave a parley, to confer with him.   130

A parley sounded. Enter Reignier on the walls.

     See, Reignier, see, thy daughter prisoner!

Reig. To whom?

Suf.   To me.

Reig.   Suffolk, what remedy?
     I am a soldier and unapt to weep
     Or to exclaim on fortune's fickleness.

Suf. Yes, there is remedy enough, my lord.   135
     Consent, and for thy honour give consent,
     Thy daughter shall be wedded to my king,
     Whom I with pain have woo'd and won thereto;

And this her easy-held imprisonment
Hath gain'd thy daughter princely liberty.   140

Reig. Speaks Suffolk as he thinks?

Suf.   Fair Margaret knows
That Suffolk doth not flatter, face, or feign.

Reig. Upon thy princely warrant, I descend
To give thee answer of thy just demand.

                           [Exit from the walls.]

Suf. And here I will expect thy coming.   145

    Trumpets sound.   Enter Reignier [below].

Reig. Welcome, brave earl, into our territories!
Command in Anjou what your honour pleases.

Suf. Thanks, Reignier, happy for so sweet a child,
Fit to be made companion with a king.
What answer makes your Grace unto my suit?   150

Reig. Since thou dost deign to woo her little worth
To be the princely bride of such a lord;
Upon condition I may quietly
Enjoy mine own, the country Maine and Anjou,
Free from oppression or the stroke of war,   155
My daughter shall be Henry's, if he please.

Suf. That is her ransom; I deliver her;
And those two counties I will undertake
Your Grace shall well and quietly enjoy.

Reig. And I again, in Henry's royal name,   160
As deputy unto that gracious king,
Give thee her hand, for sign of plighted faith.

Suf. Reignier of France, I give thee kingly thanks,
    Because this is in traffic of a king.
    [*Aside.*] And yet, methinks, I could be well
        content   165
    To be mine own attorney in this case.
    I'll over then to England with this news,
    And make this marriage to be solemniz'd.
    So farewell, Reignier! Set this diamond safe
    In golden palaces, as it becomes.   170

Reig. I do embrace thee, as I would embrace
    The Christian prince, King Henry, were he here.

Mar. Farewell, my lord! Good wishes, praise, and
        prayers
    Shall Suffolk ever have of Margaret.   *Going.*

Suf. Farewell, sweet madam! But hark you, Mar-
        garet;   175
    No princely commendations to my king?

Mar. Such commendations as becomes a maid,
    A virgin, and his servant, say to him.

Suf. Words sweetly plac'd and modestly directed.
    But, madam, I must trouble you again;   180
    No loving token to his Majesty?

Mar. Yes, my good lord, a pure unspotted heart,
    Never yet taint with love, I send the King.

Suf. And this withal.   *Kisses her.*

Mar. That for thyself; I will not so presume   185
    To send such peevish tokens to a king.
            [*Exeunt Reignier and Margaret.*]

Suf. O, wert thou for myself !   But, Suffolk, stay,
    Thou mayst not wander in that labyrinth ;
    There Minotaurs and ugly treasons lurk.
    Solicit Henry with her wondrous praise ;   190
    Bethink thee on her virtues that surmount,
    And natural graces that extinguish art ;
    Repeat their semblance often on the seas,
    That, when thou com'st to kneel at Henry's feet,
    Thou mayst bereave him of his wits with wonder.
                                   Exit.

SCENE IV

[Camp of the Duke of York in Anjou.]

Enter York, Warwick [and others].

York. Bring forth that sorceress condemn'd to burn.

[Enter La Pucelle, guarded, and a Shepherd.]

Shep. Ah, Joan, this kills thy father's heart outright !
    Have I sought every country far and near,
    And, now it is my chance to find thee out,
    Must I behold thy timeless cruel death ?   5
    Ah, Joan, sweet daughter Joan, I'll die with thee !
Puc. Decrepit miser ! base ignoble wretch !
    I am descended of a gentler blood.
    Thou art no father nor no friend of mine.
Shep. Out, out !   My lords, an please you, 'tis not so. 10
    I did beget her, all the parish knows.

Her mother liveth yet, can testify
She was the first fruit of my bachelorship.

War. Graceless ! wilt thou deny thy parentage ?

York. This argues what her kind of life hath been,   15
Wicked and vile ; and so her death concludes.

Shep. Fie, Joan, that thou wilt be so obstacle !
God knows thou art a collop of my flesh,
And for thy sake have I shed many a tear.
Deny me not, I prithee, gentle Joan.   20

Puc. Peasant, avaunt ! — You have suborn'd this man,
Of purpose to obscure my noble birth.

Shep. 'Tis true, I gave a noble to the priest
The morn that I was wedded to her mother.   24
Kneel down and take my blessing, good my girl.
Wilt thou not stoop ?   Now cursed be the time
Of thy nativity !   I would the milk
Thy mother gave thee when thou suck'dst her
    breast,
Had been a little ratsbane for thy sake !
Or else, when thou didst keep my lambs a-field,   30
I wish some ravenous wolf had eaten thee !
Dost thou deny thy father, cursed drab ?
O, burn her, burn her ! hanging is too good.

Exit.

York. Take her away ; for she hath liv'd too long,
To fill the world with vicious qualities.   35

Puc. First, let me tell you whom you have condemn'd :
Not me begotten of a shepherd swain,

But issued from the progeny of kings ;
Virtuous and holy ; chosen from above,
By inspiration of celestial grace,   40
To work exceeding miracles on earth.
I never had to do with wicked spirits ;
But you, that are polluted with your lusts,
Stain'd with the guiltless blood of innocents,
Corrupt and tainted with a thousand vices,   45
Because you want the grace that others have,
You judge it straight a thing impossible
To compass wonders but by help of devils.
No ; misconceived ! Joan of Arc hath been
A virgin from her tender infancy,   50
Chaste and immaculate in very thought ;
Whose maiden blood, thus rigorously effus'd,
Will cry for vengeance at the gates of heaven.

York. Ay, ay ; away with her to execution !

War. And hark ye, sirs ; because she is a maid,   55
Spare for no faggots, let there be enow.
Place barrels of pitch upon the fatal stake,
That so her torture may be shortened.

Puc. Will nothing turn your unrelenting hearts ?
Then, Joan, discover thine infirmity,   60
That warranteth by law to be thy privilege.
I am with child, ye bloody homicides !
Murder not then the fruit within my womb,
Although ye hale me to a violent death.

York. Now heaven forfend ! the holy maid with child ! 65

War. The greatest miracle that e'er ye wrought!
    Is all your strict preciseness come to this?

York. She and the Dauphin have been juggling.
    I did imagine what would be her refuge.

War. Well, go to; we'll have no bastards live,   70
    Especially since Charles must father it.

Puc. You are deceiv'd; my child is none of his.
    It was Alençon that enjoy'd my love.

York. Alençon! that notorious Machiavel!
    It dies, an if it had a thousand lives.   75

Puc. O, give me leave, I have deluded you.
    'Twas neither Charles nor yet the duke I nam'd,
    But Reignier, King of Naples, that prevail'd.

War. A married man! that's most intolerable.

York. Why, here's a girl! I think she knows not
    well,   80
    There were so many, whom she may accuse.

War. It's sign she hath been liberal and free.

York. And yet, forsooth, she is a virgin pure.
    Strumpet, thy words condemn thy brat and thee.
    Use no entreaty, for it is in vain.   85

Puc. Then lead me hence; with whom I leave my curse:
    May never glorious sun reflex his beams
    Upon the country where you make abode,
    But darkness and the gloomy shade of death
    Environ you, till mischief and despair   90
    Drive you to break your necks or hang your-
    selves!   *Exit [guarded].*

I

York. Break thou in pieces and consume to ashes,
    Thou foul accursed minister of hell !

Enter Cardinal [Beaufort, Bishop of Winchester, attended].

Car. Lord Regent, I do greet your excellence
    With letters of commission from the King.   95
    For know, my lords, the states of Christen-
        dom,
    Mov'd with remorse of these outrageous broils,
    Have earnestly implor'd a general peace
    Betwixt our nation and the aspiring French ;
    And here at hand the Dauphin and his train   100
    Approacheth, to confer about some matter.
York. Is all our travail turn'd to this effect ?
    After the slaughter of so many peers,
    So many captains, gentlemen, and soldiers,
    That in this quarrel have been overthrown   105
    And sold their bodies for their country's benefit,
    Shall we at last conclude effeminate peace ?
    Have we not lost most part of all the towns,
    By treason, falsehood, and by treachery,
    Our great progenitors had conquered ?   110
    O, Warwick, Warwick ! I foresee with grief
    The utter loss of all the realm of France.
War. Be patient, York. If we conclude a peace,
    It shall be with such strict and severe covenants
    As little shall the Frenchmen gain thereby.   115

Enter Charles, Alençon, Bastard, Reignier [and others].

Char. Since, lords of England, it is thus agreed
    That peaceful truce shall be proclaim'd in France,
    We come to be informed by yourselves
    What the conditions of that league must be.
York. Speak, Winchester; for boiling choler chokes 120
    The hollow passage of my poison'd voice,
    By sight of these our baleful enemies.
Car. Charles, and the rest, it is enacted thus:
    That, in regard King Henry gives consent,
    Of mere compassion and of lenity,   125
    To ease your country of distressful war,
    And suffer you to breathe in fruitful peace,
    You shall become true liegemen to his crown;
    And, Charles, upon condition thou wilt swear
    To pay him tribute and submit thyself,   130
    Thou shalt be plac'd as viceroy under him,
    And still enjoy thy regal dignity.
Alen. Must he be then as shadow of himself?
    Adorn his temples with a coronet,
    And yet, in substance and authority,   135
    Retain but privilege of a private man?
    This proffer is absurd and reasonless.
Char. 'Tis known already that I am possess'd
    With more than half the Gallian territories,
    And therein reverenc'd for their lawful king: 140
    Shall I, for lucre of the rest unvanquish'd,

Detract so much from that prerogative
As to be call'd but viceroy of the whole?
No, lord ambassador, I'll rather keep
That which I have than, coveting for more,   145
Be cast from possibility of all.

York. Insulting Charles! hast thou by secret means
Used intercession to obtain a league,
And, now the matter grows to compromise,
Stand'st thou aloof upon comparison?   150
Either accept the title thou usurp'st,
Of benefit proceeding from our king
And not of any challenge of desert,
Or we will plague thee with incessant wars.

Reig. My lord, you do not well in obstinacy   155
To cavil in the course of this contract.
If once it be neglected, ten to one
We shall not find like opportunity.

Alen. To say the truth, it is your policy
To save your subjects from such massacre   160
And ruthless slaughters as are daily seen
By our proceeding in hostility;
And therefore take this compact of a truce,
Although you break it when your pleasure serves.

War. How say'st thou, Charles? Shall our condition
          stand?   165

Char. It shall;
Only reserv'd, you claim no interest
In any of our towns of garrison.

York. Then swear allegiance to his Majesty,
      As thou art knight, never to disobey   170
      Nor be rebellious to the crown of England,
      Thou, nor thy nobles, to the crown of England.
                 [*Charles and his party give signs of fealty.*]
      So, now dismiss your army when ye please ;
      Hang up your ensigns, let your drums be still,
      For here we entertain a solemn peace.   175
                                 Exeunt.

SCENE V

[*London.   The palace.*]

*Enter Suffolk in conference with the King; Gloucester
            and Exeter [following].*

King. Your wondrous rare description, noble earl,
      Of beauteous Margaret hath astonish'd me.
      Her virtues graced with external gifts
      Do breed love's settled passions in my heart ;
      And like as rigour of tempestuous gusts   5
      Provokes the mightiest hulk against the tide,
      So am I driven by breath of her renown
      Either to suffer shipwreck or arrive
      Where I may have fruition of her love.
Suf. Tush, my good lord, this superficial tale   10
      Is but a preface of her worthy praise.
      The chief perfections of that lovely dame,
      Had I sufficient skill to utter them,

Would make a volume of enticing lines,
Able to ravish any dull conceit;   15
And, which is more, she is not so divine,
So full-replete with choice of all delights,
But with as humble lowliness of mind
She is content to be at your command;
Command, I mean, of virtuous chaste intents,   20
To love and honour Henry as her lord.

King. And otherwise will Henry ne'er presume.
Therefore, my Lord Protector, give consent
That Margaret may be England's royal queen.

Glou. So should I give consent to flatter sin.   25
You know, my lord, your Highness is betroth'd
Unto another lady of esteem.
How shall we then dispense with that contract,
And not deface your honour with reproach?

Suf. As doth a ruler with unlawful oaths;   30
Or one that, at a triumph having vow'd
To try his strength, forsaketh yet the lists
By reason of his adversary's odds.
A poor earl's daughter is unequal odds,
And therefore may be broke without offence.   35

Glou. Why, what, I pray, is Margaret more than that?
Her father is no better than an earl,
Although in glorious titles he excel.

Suf. Yes, my lord, her father is a king,
The King of Naples and Jerusalem;   40
And of such great authority in France

As his alliance will confirm our peace
And keep the Frenchmen in allegiance.

Glou. And so the Earl of Armagnac may do,
Because he is near kinsman unto Charles.   45

Exe. Beside, his wealth doth warrant a liberal dower,
Where Reignier sooner will receive than give.

Suf. A dower, my lords ! disgrace not so your king,
That he should be so abject, base, and poor,
To choose for wealth and not for perfect love.   50
Henry is able to enrich his queen
And not to seek a queen to make him rich.
So worthless peasants bargain for their wives,
As market-men for oxen, sheep, or horse.
Marriage is a matter of more worth   55
Than to be dealt in by attorneyship.
Not whom we will, but whom his Grace affects,
Must be companion of his nuptial bed.
And therefore, lords, since he affects her most,
[It] most of all these reasons bindeth us,   60
In our opinions she should be preferr'd.
For what is wedlock forced but a hell,
An age of discord and continual strife ?
Whereas the contrary bringeth bliss,
And is a pattern of celestial peace.   65
Whom should we match with Henry, being a king,
But Margaret, that is daughter to a king ?
Her peerless feature, joined with her birth,
Approves her fit for none but for a king.

Her valiant courage and undaunted spirit,   70
More than in women commonly is seen,
Will answer our hope in issue of a king;
For Henry, son unto a conqueror,
Is likely to beget more conquerors,
If with a lady of so high resolve   75
As is fair Margaret he be link'd in love.
Then yield, my lords; and here conclude with me
That Margaret shall be Queen, and none but she.

King. Whether it be through force of your report,
My noble Lord of Suffolk, or for that   80
My tender youth was never yet attaint
With any passion of inflaming love,
I cannot tell; but this I am assur'd,
I feel such sharp dissension in my breast,
Such fierce alarums both of hope and fear,   85
As I am sick with working of my thoughts.
Take, therefore, shipping; post, my lord, to
    France;
Agree to any covenants, and procure
That Lady Margaret do vouchsafe to come
To cross the seas to England and be crown'd   90
King Henry's faithful and anointed queen.
For your expenses and sufficient charge,
Among the people gather up a tenth.
Be gone, I say; for, till you do return,
I rest perplexed with a thousand cares.   95
And you, good uncle, banish all offence.

If you do censure me by what you were,
Not what you are, I know it will excuse
This sudden execution of my will.
And so, conduct me where, from company,   100
I may revolve and ruminate my grief.   *Exit.*

Glou. Ay, grief, I fear me, both at first and last.

                      Exeunt Gloucester [and Exeter].

Suf. Thus Suffolk hath prevail'd ; and thus he goes,
As did the youthful Paris once to Greece,
With hope to find the like event in love,   105
But prosper better than the Troyan did.
Margaret shall now be Queen, and rule the King ;
But I will rule both her, the King, and realm.

                                Exit.

Notes

A list of *Dramatis Personæ* was first added, imperfectly, by Rowe in 1709. The corrected list dates from Clark and Wright, 1864.

Act First. Scene i. Acts I and II are not divided into scenes in the Folio; Act III is divided as in the text; Act IV has but two scenes, the second beginning with Act V of the text. Act V in the Folio begins at V. v. The accepted division is due to modern editors.

I. i. 1. **Hung be the heavens with black.** On the Elizabethan stage the roof or upper part, called the "heavens," was draped with black when a tragedy was enacted.

I. i. 27. **By magic verses.** Referring to the medieval belief that death could be effected through metrical incantation. See Spenser's "inchaunted rimes," *Faerie Queene*, I. ix. 48.

I. i. 56. **or bright —.** Pope supplied "Francis Drake," to complete the comparison and a couplet as well. Many other conjectures have been made, more plausible than the name of a man then living. Perhaps the printer could not make out the name in the MS.; or perhaps the speech was meant to be represented as interrupted by the coming of the messenger.

I. i. 60. **Rheims.** This name, spelt *Rheimes* in the Ff, is treated metrically as a dissyllable.

I. i. 65. **Rouen.** Written "Roan" in the Ff, and seemingly so pronounced.

123

I. i. 131. **Fastolfe.** The Ff have *Falstaffe*. Though often accused of cowardice, the Sir John Fastolfe of the French wars seems really to have been a brave man. He died at Caister by Yarmouth in 1459. The Sir John Falstaffe of the *Henry IV* plays is not an anachronistic derivative of the " coward knight " of this play, but seems partly the embodiment of tradition concerning another Sir John Fastolfe, of Nacton, living in the reign of Henry IV. See Introductions, *1 and 2 Henry IV*, " The Tudor Shakespeare."

I. i. 132, 133. Fastolfe was perhaps in the front line of his own troops, which were placed in reserve of the van, led probably by Talbot himself.

I. i. 154. **Saint George's feast.** Held April 23, at this period.

I. i. 170. **Eltham.** Then a favorite royal palace in Kent.

I. i. 175. **Jack out of office.** Old phrase occurring in Heywood's *Proverbs* (1546) and elsewhere.

I. ii. 1. **Mars his true moving.** Referring to the difficulties in understanding the movements of Mars, before Kepler published his discoveries in 1609.

I. ii. 9. **bull-beeves.** Eating bull-beef was supposed to be productive of courage.

I. ii. 30. **Olivers and Rolands.** These most famous of Charlemagne's twelve peers were proverbial exponents of deeds of prowess.

I. ii. 56. **nine sibyls.** There were nine sibylline books offered for sale by the Cumæan Sibyl. In popular belief there had perhaps come to be nine sibyls also.

I. ii. 105. **sword of Deborah.** See *Judges* iv.

I. ii. 108. **thy.** Of thee.

I. ii. 131. **Expect Saint Martin's summer**. Expect summer in late autumn. Saint Martin's day is November 11.

I. ii. 138, 139. Probably suggested by a passage in North's Translation of Plutarch's *Life of Julius Cæsar*.

I. ii. 140. **Mahomet . . . dove**. Raleigh's *Historie of the World* tells (I. i. vi) that Mahomet had a dove, — " which he used to feed with wheat out of his ear; which dove, when it was hungry, lighted on Mahomet's shoulder, and thrust its bill in to find its breakfast; Mahomet persuading the rude and simple Arabians that it was the Holy Ghost that gave him advice."

I. ii. 143. **Saint Philip's daughters**. The four daughters of Philip mentioned *Acts* xxi, 9.

I. iii. 35. **indulgences to sin**. The bishop of Winchester had jurisdiction over the public stews. Hart mentions as passed in 1162 an Act called " ordinances touching the government of the stewholders in Southwark, under the direction of the Bishop of Winchester."

I. iii. 39. Referring to the ancient belief, " And in that place where Damascus was founded, Kaym sloughe Abell his brother," Mandeville's *Travels*, ed. 1725.

I. iii. 47. **Blue coats to tawny coats**. Blue was the ordinary color of the livery of serving men. Coats of a yellowish-dark color were the distinctive garb of ecclesiastical apparitors.

I. iii. 53. **Winchester goose**. Cant term for a disease likely to be contracted in the places referred to in note on l. 35.

I. iii. 53. **a rope! a rope!** A cry of abuse often taught to parrots.

I. iii. 84. **call for clubs.** This was originally the call to rouse the apprentices, who used clubs as weapons, to take part in a street affray.

I. iv. 95. **Plantagenet.** Salisbury's real name was Montacute.

I. iv. 107. **dolphin or dogfish.** *Dolphin* is the old form of *dauphin.* The word is so written in the Ff. The dogfish was especially hated, and the name used as a term of abuse.

I. v. 6. **Blood will I draw.** To draw a witch's blood was the accredited method to become immune from her power.

I. v. 21. **like Hannibal.** With reference to Hannibal's stratagem to escape by fixing lighted twigs on the horns of oxen, told in Livy, xxii, c. 16.

I. v. 31. **leopard.** Trisyllabic here. So *English* in vi. 2, below.

I. vi. 6. **Adonis' garden.** The tradition of these gardens, unknown in classical antiquity, was widespread in Shakespeare's day. See Spenser's *Faerie Queene*, III. vi. 29.

I. vi. 22. **Rhodope's or Memphis'.** Rhodope was a famous courtesan, a Greek, born a slave, said to have built with her wealth a pyramid near Memphis. One tradition tells that she afterward married Psammeticus, King of Egypt. Capell plausibly conjectures the reading, "Rhodope of Memphis." Landor's *Imaginary Conversations* includes a dialogue between Æsop and Rhodope.

II. i. 8. **dead march.** They are bringing Salisbury in funeral procession. See ii. 4.

II. iii. 6. **Scythian Tomyris.** Queen of the Massagetæ,

who after her husband's death killed Cyrus with her own hand (538 B.C.).

II. iii. 36. shadow. Here image or portrait, as often in Shakespeare. Possibly the Countess had been " practising " on Talbot's waxen image, as in the witchcraft of the time. See 45–47.

II. iv. This Warwick was Richard Beauchamp, Lieutenant Governor and General of France, dying in 1439. He appears in *Henry V.* The Warwick of Parts II and III is the more famous Richard Nevil, the " setter up and puller down of kings," Earl of Warwick in right of his marriage to Richard Beauchamp's daughter (1449).

II. iv. 83. grandfather. Malone pointed out that Clarence was really Plantagenet's maternal great-great grandfather.

II. iv. 86. bears him on . . . privilege. He presumes on the privileges of the Temple Grounds. It does not appear, however, that the Temple, then as now the residence of law students, had privileges of Sanctuary.

II. v. Edmund Mortimer served in the French wars of Henry V, dying at home in Ireland in 1424. His uncle, Sir John Mortimer, with whom he is perhaps confused here, was imprisoned in the Tower and executed.

II. v. 74. mother. Should be *grandmother*, strictly.

III. The Parliament at the opening of this Act was held in 1426 at Leicester, not at London as here represented. Historically Warwick was not present, but was in France.

III. i. 42. bastard. Winchester was the illegitimate son of John of Gaunt and Katherine Swynford, who were afterward married.

III. i. 51. Roam thither. There are also quibbles on

Rome and *room* in Shakespeare, possible since the earlier *Rome* shifted its pronunciation into *Room* in this period. *Room* has now been antiquated for many decades, the older sound being restored, probably by influence of the spelling.

III. i. 78. **Bishop.** Meaning *bishop's*, *i.e.* the bishop's men.

III. i. 99. **inkhorn mate.** Bookish fellow, scribbling chap. Used contemptuously.

III. i. 102. **parings of our nails.** In a "pitched field" sharp stakes were set up to protect footmen from the enemy's cavalry. The meaning is that almost anything pointed would do, were stakes not found.

III. ii. The strategy used in the capture of Rouen is not historic, but is perhaps based on a similar story told by the chroniclers of the capture of the castle of Cornill (1441).

III. ii. 25. **To that.** Compared to that.

III. ii. 30. **burning torch.** The suggestion for this "beacon" came perhaps from an incident in the betrayal of Le Mans to the French.

III. ii. 64. **Hecate.** Trisyllabic here, though generally dissyllabic in Shakespeare.

III. ii. 67. **Signior, no.** An old remark of stock repartee, another form of which is "signior si." See Bullen's *Old Plays*, I. 325, and note.

III. ii. 83. **Cœur-de-lion's heart.** The reference to the burial of the heart of Richard I at Rouen is from Holinshed.

III. ii. 95. **Pendragon.** Uther Pendragon was the father of King Arthur. This story of the litter is in Hardyng, but in Holinshed is told of Pendragon's brother.

III. ii. 102. **out of hand.** Forthwith, directly.

III. ii. 126. **take some order.** Make necessary arrangements.

III. iii. 72. **set him free.** " The Duke [of Orleans] was not liberated till *after* Burgundy's decline to the French . . . nor was that during the regency of York, but of Bedford." — RITSON.

III. iii. 85. **like a Frenchman.** The slur on the inconstancy of the French is much out of place in the mouth of Joan.

III. iv. 18. **I do remember.** " Henry was but nine months old when his father died, and never saw him." — MALONE.

III. iv. 38. **law of arms.** Blackstone's *Commentaries* says on this point : —

" By the ancient law before the Conquest, fighting in the king's palace, or before the king's judges, was punished with death . . . malicious striking in the king's palace, whereby blood is drawn is punishable by perpetual imprisonment and fine at the king's pleasure, and also with loss of the offender's right hand."

IV. i. 19. **Poictiers.** The *Poictiers* of the Ff was corrected by Capell to *Patay*, as in the chronicles. Poictiers was fought in 1357, Patay in 1428.

IV. ii. 48. **In blood.** In good condition. A sportsman's term.

IV. ii. 49. **rascal-like.** Like lean and worthless deer. *Rascal* meant a deer not worth killing. The usage here is from Holinshed.

IV. iii. Historically York and Somerset were in England at this time, not participating in the French wars.

K

IV. iii. 47. **vulture.** A metaphor drawn obviously from the Prometheus myth.

IV. iii. 51. **ever living man of memory.** Man of ever living memory.

IV. iv. 19. **in advantage ling'ring.** " Protracting his resistance by the advantage of a strong post." — JOHNSON.

IV. v. 22. **your regard.** Regard for your own preservation.

IV. vi. 3. **France his sword.** The King of France's sword.

IV. vi. 15. **pride of Gallia.** Full power of France.

IV. vi. 44. **On that advantage.** For the sake of the advantages you mention, *i.e.* to preserve our household name, etc.

IV. vi. 54-55. **sire of Crete.** Dædalus. Reference to the story of Icarus occurs also in vii. 15-16.

IV. vii. 10. **Tend'ring my ruin.** Protecting me in my extremity.

IV. vii. 63. This list of Talbot's titles is not given in the chronicles. The exact source for it here is unknown.

IV. vii. 73. **Turk.** Probably a reference to the " silly stately " account of the Turk Bajazeth's dignities in Marlowe's *Tamburlaine*, Part I, III. i, etc.

V. i. 28-29. **install'd . . . cardinal.** For the inconsistency here, and in ii. 2, below, see Introduction.

V. iii. 6. **monarch of the north.** Evil spirits were supposed to come from the north. This scene with the fiends and the later Joan scenes, save that with her father, are built on assertions in Holinshed.

V. iii. 71. **makes the senses rough.** Perhaps makes dull or ruffles the senses. The line may be corrupt, and has been frequently amended.

V. iii. 84. **cooling card.** A card so decisive as to check or moderate an adversary's courage. The expression was popular with Lyly and others.

V. iii. 109. **I cry you mercy.** I beg your pardon.

V. iii. 109. **quid for quo.** One thing for another.

V. iv. 68. **juggling.** A trisyllable.

V. iv. 74. **Machiavel.** The reference is anachronistic here, since Machiavelli's *Il Principe* was not published till 1513. Elizabethan literature abounds in references to Machiavelli as the incarnation of wickedness.

V. iv. 152. **of benefit.** Explained by Johnson as meaning, " Be content to live as the beneficiary of our King." Law term.

V. v. 64. **contrary.** Ff 2, 3, 4 add " forth." *Contrary* was probably pronounced as a quadrisyllable, *conterary.*

V. v. 93. **tenth.** A fifteenth in the chronicles.

Textual Variants

The text in the present edition is based upon the first Folio, and the following list records the more important variations from that version.

I. i.   49. moist] F$_2$; moistned F$_1$.
         50. marish] Pope; nourish F.
         65. [Is Rouen] is Roan F$_1$, and is Roan F$_2$.
         83. their] Theobald; her F.
    92, etc. Dauphin] Dolphin F.
        176. steal] Singer; send F.
    ii. 30. bred] Rowe; breed F.
        37. hare-brain'd] Dyce; hair-brain'd F.
   iv. 33. vile] Cambridge; pil'd F.
        95. like thee [Nero] Malone; like thee F$_1$; Nero-like will F$_2$.

II. i.   29. all together] Rowe; altogether F.
   iv. 1, etc. *Plan] Yorke* F.
        76. faction] fashion F.
        117. wip'd] F$_2$; whipt F$_1$.
    v. 71. King] F$_2$; F$_1$ omits.

III. i. 52–55. *Rearranged from Ff. by Theobald.*
        163. alone] F^2; all alone F$_1$.
    ii. 13. *Qui est là?*] Malone; che la F.
        14. Paysans pauvres] Rowe; Peasauns la pouure F.

IV. i.   48. my Lord] F$_2$; Lord F$_1$.
        180. wist] wish F.
   iii. 17, etc. [*Lucy*] 2 *Mes.* F.
    iv. 16. legions] Rowe; regions F.
   vii. 94. them what] F$_2$; him F$_1$.

V. iii. 57. her wings] F$_2$; his wings F$_1$.
        192. And] Capell; Mad F$_1$; Made F$_2$.
    v. 59. her] Cambridge; F omits.

Glossary

accidents, events, occurrences; V. iii. 4.
accomplices, associates (in good sense); V. ii. 9.
admonish, notify, inform; V. iii. 3.
advance, lift up; I. vi. 1.
advantage, favorable opportunity; II. v. 129.
affects, is drawn to, likes; V. v. 57.
agaz'd on, astonished, amazed at; I. i. 126.
Alcides, Hercules; IV. vii. 60.
alliance, relationship; II. v. 53.
amaze, terrify; IV. vii. 84.
amort, spiritless, dejected; III. ii. 124.
antic, buffoon; IV. vii. 18.
apprehension, opinion, conception of; II. iv. 102.
argue, show, prove; II. v. 7.
argument, token, evidence; V. i. 46.
arms, coat of arms; I. i. 80.
as, that; III. i. 16.
Astræa, goddess of justice (quadrisyllabic); I. vi. 4.
attached, seized, arrested; II. iv. 96.
attainted, condemned to the penalties and forfeitures attaching to treason; II. iv. 96.
attorneyship, proxyship; V. v. 56.

banning, cursing; V. iii. 42.
bearing-cloth, a child's christening robe; I. iii. 42.
bestow, dispose of, lodge; III. ii. 88.
bewray'd, disclosed, made known; IV. i. 107.
bill, statement of accusations; III. i.
boot, profit, use; IV. vi. 52.

bow, leave the field; IV. v. 29.

brandish, let flash and glitter, like a brandished sword
  I. i. 3.

break, disclose; I. iii. 81.

break up, break open; I. iii. 13.

broach, tap (as a cask), let out, shed; III. iv. 39.

bruited, rumored, announced as with a noise; II. iii. 68

buckle with, grapple or close with; I. ii. 95.

canker, canker-worm; II. iv. 68.

canvass, toss in a blanket, in punishment or sport; I. iii. 36.

cap, cardinal's hat; V. i. 33.

captivate, captive, taken prisoner; II. iii. 42.

cates, delicacies; II. iii. 79.

censure, opinion, judgment; II. iii. 10.

censure, estimate, judge; V. v. 97.

certified, informed, made certain; IV. i. 144.

challenge, claim; V. iv. 153.

charge, cost, expense; V. v. 92.

cheer, countenance, face; I. ii. 48.

circumstance, details, particulars; I. i. 109.

coat, coat of arms; I. i. 81.

cognizance, badge; II. iv. 108.

collop, piece of flesh; V. iv. 18.

commandment, command (quadrisyllabic); I. iii. 20.

conceit, invention, ingenuity embodied in something devised; IV. i. 102: understanding, intelligence; V. v. 15.

concluded of, concluded on, agreed upon or arranged;
  V. i. 5.

consented unto, acted in concert to bring about; I. i. 5.

contemptible, lowly, mean; I. ii. 75.

contrarieties, contradictions; II. iii. 59.

conveyance, trickery, underhand dealing; I. iii. 2.

cornets, cavalry, horsemen; IV. iii. 25.

corrosive, fretting (initial accent); III. iii. 3.

crazy, infirm, decrepit; III. ii. 89.

credit, honorable reputation; IV. i. 36.

crestless, ignoble, having no right to bear coat armor; II. iv. 85.

darnel, an injurious weed, thought to be harmful to the eyes; III. ii. 44.

dearest, most precious; III. iv. 40.

decipher'd, disclosed; IV. i. 184.

default, fault; II. i. 60.

devise on, think, decide on; I. ii. 124.

diffidence, distrust, suspicion; III. iii. 10.

digest, dispose of, vent; IV. i. 167.

dignities, dignitaries; I. iii. 50.

disable, depreciate, disparage; V. iii. 67.

disanimates, discourages, disheartens; III. i. 183.

discover, reveal, tell; II. v. 59.

disease, dis-ease, trouble; II. v. 44.

dismay not, be not dismayed; III. iii. 1.

distrain'd, confiscated, annexed; I. iii. 61.

drooping chair, chair fit for old age; IV. v. 5.

due, invest, endow; IV. ii. 34.

effus'd, shed; V. iv. 52.

emulation, factious or envious rivalry; IV. iv. 21.

endamage, damage, injure; II. i. 77.

enlargement, release; II. v. 30.

enrank, place in ranks; I. i. 115.

entertain, come under obligations in regard to, allow to enter; V. iv. 175.

entertain'd, treated in general; I. iv. 38.

envy, spite, malice; IV. i. 193.

espials, scouts, spies; I. iv. 8.

exempt, excluded, removed; II. iv. 93.

exequies, funeral rites, obsequies; III. ii. 133.

exigent, decisive moment, end; II. v. 9.

expuls'd, driven out, expelled; III. iii. 25.

extirped, rooted out, extirpated; III. iii. 24.

extremes, straits, " most extremes," greatest extremities of danger; IV. i. 38.

face, show a false face, play the hypocrite; V. iii. 142.

fact, evil deed, crime; IV. i. 30.

familiar, familiar spirit or demon; III. ii. 122.

fancy, love; V. iii. 91.

feature, bodily shape, or general appearance; V. v. 68.

flesh, use for the first time; IV. vii. 36.

flower-de-luce, the heraldic lily, the emblem of France; I. i. 80.

fond, foolish; II. iii. 45.

foot-boys, lackeys; III. ii. 69.

forged, contrived, devised; IV. i. 102.

forlorn, wretched, referring to former bad fortune; I. ii. 19.

forth, forth from, from out; I. ii. 54.

fortitude, vigor, strength; II. i. 17.

fortune, fate; IV. iv. 39.

guard, court of, station occupied by soldiers on guard; II. i. 4.

giglot, wanton; IV. vii. 41.

gimmers, connecting parts or contrivances in clockwork (*Gimmalls,* Ff 2, 3, 4); I. ii. 41.

gird, a rebuke or twit; III. i. 131.

gleeks, mocks or gibes (*glikes* Ff); III. ii. 123.

Goliases, Goliahs or Goliaths; I. ii. 33.

guardant, defender, sentinel; IV. vii. 9.

Glossary

halcyon, old name of kingfisher; " halcyon days " here are calm days (Ff 1, 2, *Hacyons days*); I. ii. 131.

hale, drag, or pull (on a rope); I. i. 149.

have with thee (imperative), let us go; idiomatical use announcing the speaker's intention to go somewhere; II. iv. 114.

head, armed force, army; I. iv. 100.

heart-blood, heart's blood; I. iii. 83.

homicide, manslayer; I. ii. 25.

hungry prey, prey for their hunger; I. ii. 28.

immanity, atrocious ferocity; V. i. 13.

infus'd, shed or diffused; I. ii. 85.

inhearsed, inclosed as in a coffin; IV. vii. 45.

inshipp'd, provided with ships; V. i. 49.

insulting, exulting; I. ii. 138.

intermissive, coming at intervals; I. i. 88.

latter, last; II. v. 38.

lead, lining of wooden coffin; I. i. 64.

lie, sojourn, dwell; III. ii. 129.

lift, lifted; I. i. 16.

like, liken, compare; IV. vi. 48.

linstock, staff holding the gunner's match; I. iv. 56.

lither, supple, soft; IV. vii. 21.

long of, all along of, owing to; IV. iii. 33.

lowly, lying low (in death); III. iii. 47.

lowted, treated with contumely, mocked; IV. iii. 13.

malice, enmity, ill will; III. i. 128; IV. i. 108.

marish, marsh (Pope's conjecture for Ff *nourish*); I. i. 50.

mean, medium, moderation; I. ii. 121.

mean, means; III. ii. 10.

merchant, fellow (contemptuous use); II. iii. 57.
method, order followed in writing; III. i. 13.
mickle, great, much; IV. vi. 35.
Minotaurs, the minotaur was the fabled monster in the Cretan labyrinth; V. iii. 189.
misconceived, having a mistaken idea, or misconception; V. iv. 49.
miser, wretched person; V. iv. 7.
mortality, death; IV. v. 32.
motion, proposal, counsel; V. i. 7.
mouth, bark, cry; II. iv. 12.
munition, ammunition; I. i. 168.
muse, marvel, wonder; II. ii. 19.

neglection, neglect; IV. iii. 49.
nephew, cousin (as often in Shakespeare); II. v. 64.
Nestor-like, like Nestor, oldest and wisest of the Homeric heroes; II. v. 6.
noble, a gold coin of the value of 6s. 8d.; V. iv. 23.
nonce, for the, as occasion requires; II. iii. 57.

objected, proposed, brought forward; II. iv. 43.
obstacle, a vulgar corruption of *obstinate;* V. iv. 17.
ordnance, a small gun, cannon; I. iv. 15.
otherwhiles, at times, now and then; I. ii. 7.
overpeer, look down on; I. iv. 11.

packing, be, away with you; IV. i. 46.
Paris-ward, unto, to Paris; III. iii. 30.
partaker, supporter, confederate; II. iv. 100.
parties, parts, sides; V. ii. 12.
parting, departing; II. v. 115.
party, part, side; II. iv. 32.

patronage, to protect, maintain; III. i. 48.

peel'd, tonsured, shaven; I. iii. 30.

peevish, senseless, foolish; II. iv. 76.

periapts, inscribed amulets or charms; V. iii. 2.

period, consummation, end; IV. ii. 17.

peruse, scrutinize, scan; IV. ii. 43.

pinch, slight bite, or snap; IV. ii. 49.

pitch, term in falconry for height to which hawk soars before stooping; II. iii. 55.

platforms, designs, schemes; II. i. 77.

policies, stratagems, tricks; III. iii. 12.

post, hasten, speed; V. v. 87.

practisants, contrivers, fellow plotters; III. ii. 20.

practise, use stratagems, plot; II. i. 25.

preferr'd, brought forward, presented; III. i. 10.

present, immediate; III. iv. 39.

presently, immediately; I. ii. 149.

pretend, plan, intend; IV. i. 6.

pretend, indicate, portend; IV. i. 54.

prevented, anticipated; IV. i. 71.

proditor, betrayer, traitor; I. iii. 31.

proper, comely, handsome; V. iii. 37.

provokes, impels; V. v. 6.

purblind, half blind, short or dim-sighted; II. iv. 21.

pursuivants, state messengers, inferior heralds; II. v. 5.

puzzel, hussy, drab (a form of *pucelle*); I. iv. 107.

pyramis, pyramid (Latin form); I. vi. 21.

quaint, clever, ingenious; IV. i. 102.

quell, destroy, slay; I. i. 163.

Qui est la? Who is there? III. ii. 13.

quillets, fine distinctions, subtleties; II. iv. 17.

quittance, repay, retaliate; II. i. 14.

rearward, rearguard; III. iii. 33.

reflex, throw or cast beams; V. iv. 87.

reguerdon, recompense, reward; III. i. 170.

remorse, relenting, pity; V. iv. 97.

repugn, withstand, reject; IV. i. 94.

resolve on, be sure of; I. ii. 91.

resolved, assured, satisfied; III. iv. 20.

rive, fire till they split; IV. ii. 29.

Saint Denis, the patron saint of France; I. vi. 28.

scruple, perplexity; V. iii. 93.

seal'd up, brought to a determination, completed; I. i. 130.

secure, heedless, confiding; II. i. 11.

sennet, a particular set of notes on a trumpet; III. i. 186.

servitors, soldiers; those serving in wars; II. i. 5.

shot, picked gunners, marksmen; I. iv. 53.

significants, tokens or indications, signs; II. iv. 26.

sirrah, used in addressing inferiors; III. i. 62.

smear'd, smirched, stained; IV. vii. 3.

solicit, incite, stir up; V. iii. 190.

sort, select, choose; II. iii. 27.

spleen, ardor, impetuosity; IV. vi. 13.

stablish, establish; V. i. 10.

stand, stand up to, resist; I. i. 123.

still, continually; I. iii. 63.

stomach, bitter resentments, angry tempers; I. iii. 90· appetites; II. iii. 80.

subscribe, submit, yield; II. iv. 44.

supply, troops, reinforcements; I. i. 159.

sweeting, term of endearment; III. iii. 21.

taint, tinctured or imbued; V. iii. 183.

Talbotites, contemptuous name given to the English (Theobald's emendation of the Ff *Talbonites*); III. ii. 28.

timeless, premature, untimely; V. iv. 5.
toy, idle fancy or impulse; trifle; IV. i. 145.
traffic, transaction; V. iii. 164.
train, tail; III. iii. 7.
train'd, enticed, lured; II, iii. 35.
triumph, public festivity or display; V. v. 31.
trull, harlot; II. ii. 28.

unable, weak, powerless; IV. v. 4.
unaccustom'd, unseemly, unusual; III. i. 93.
unavoided, unavoidable; IV. v. 8.
unfallible, infallible, certain; I. ii. 59.
unkind, unnatural; IV. i. 193.
unready, not dressed, having toilet unfinished; II. i. 39.

vail, let fall, lower; V. iii. 25.
vantage, favorable condition or advantage; IV. v. 28.
vaward, vanguard, advanced guard of an army; I. i. 132.

Walloon, a dweller along the border between the Netherlands and France; I. i. 137.
warrantize, guaranty or pledge; I. iii. 13.
weening, thinking, deeming; II. v. 88.
where, whereas; V. v. 47.
whiles, until (variant of *while* or *whilst*); I. iv. 91.
will'd, bade, desired; I. ii. 80: commanded; I. iii. 10.
wist, knew; IV. i. 180.
witting, knowing; II. v. 16.
wood, mad; IV. vii. 35.
wooden, insensible, unfeeling; I. i. 19; V. iii. 89.
worthless, unworthy; IV. iv. 21.
wot, know; IV. vi. 32.
writhled, wrinkled; II. iii. 23.

yield, admit; II. iv. 42.

HONI SOIT QUI MAL Y PENSE

SEMPER EADEM